MOTOR CARRIER RATE STRUCTURES

Praeger Special Studies in

Transportation and Logistics

Grant M. Davis: Series Editor

Grant M. Davis
Eugene H. Shepard

MOTOR CARRIER RATE STRUCTURES

THE NEED FOR BASIC REVISION

PRAEGER PUBLISHERS
Praeger Special Studies

New York • London • Sydney • Toronto

PRAEGER PUBLISHERS
PRAEGER SPECIAL STUDIES
383 Madison Avenue, New York, N.Y. 10017, U.S.A.

Published in the United States of America in 1979
by Praeger Publishers,
A Division of Holt, Rinehart and Winston, CBS, Inc.

9 038 987654321

Library of Congress Catalogue Card Number: 78-24194

Printed in the United States of America

CONTENTS

Chapter | Page

LIST OF TABLES

LIST OF FIGURES

1

THE MOTOR CARRIER RATE STRUCTURE PROBLEM

PURPOSE OF THE STUDY

The significant problems of cargo loss and damage and common carrier liability are inextricable, interrelated inordinately with the troika of the small shipment problem, motor carrier profitability, and price discrimination. The Interstate Commerce Commission (ICC), through the regulatory power with which it is endowed, must "develop, coordinate and preserve a national transportation system." In this regard, the commission is charged with the comprehensive responsibility of prescribing just and reasonable rates. These rates, moreover, must avoid undue preference, prejudice, and discrimination. In accomplishing these tasks, the commission must consider by law and preserve the inherent advantage of a particular mode of transportation.[1] But the potential destruction of a carrier's inherent advantage through regulation or lack of regulation could conceivably result in substantial modification in the framework of the U.S. domestic transportation system.

The basic premise of the implication advanced here is that the motor common carrier industry appears to possess a unique, inherent transportation advantage not enjoyed by other modes of transportation. That is to say, an individual motor carrier may transport a 100,000-pound load of paper products to St. Louis, Missouri, using two trailers on any given day. On the same day, moreover, the same motor carrier may transport three trailer loads of minimum and less than truckload (LTL) shipments of all weights to the same destination, and en route deliver freight to a number of small, out-of-the-way towns.

The versatility of the motor carrier is not enjoyed by any other mode of transportation, nor does it appear that any other mode presently in existence could adequately meet the needs of the U.S. economy with the mobility and efficiency already achieved by the motor common carrier of general commodities. The ICC and the various state regulatory agencies have a serious responsibility to preserve the advantage for this mode of transportation in order to meet the dynamic needs of commerce. A reduction of the motor carrier's volume of business through unwise regulation or legislation or failure to legislate or regulate for the protection of such volume of business would bring a corresponding weakening of the entire transportation system. Rather than permit encroachment of other modes with certain regulatory advantages over the motor carrier into the field, the first step might be to equalize the regulatory advantages among the carriers within reason while simultaneously preserving as nearly as possible the inherent advantage of all.[2]

Small shipments, under the existing rate structure, are on the average being handled at a loss by motor carriers. Indeed, 75 percent of all small shipments are handled at or below cost (see Figure 1). Larger, more profitable shipments with higher rates are subsidizing the small shipment deficit. The dilemma of the motor carrier industry, however, is that the necessary volume to maintain the essential plant and equipment for a common carrier system cannot be achieved through transporting large shipments only. Motor carriers are further confounded by the erosion of larger shipment traffic volume, because of inroads made by the competition of private carriers and other modes.

If the general commodity motor carrier loses the larger LTL and truckload traffic to competitors and also loses its small shipment volume, the industry is faced with potential deficits. The most conclusive solution to the problem may be lodged within the small shipment area. For the preservation of a viable transportation system, public policy would appear to dictate that at this time motor carrier competition be restricted in terms of price competition. The approach may obviously be to restructure rates, and a simplified rating plan with limited liability, based on cost, may represent the ultimate solution to the small shipment problem.

Motor common carriers of general commodities are fully liable for the market value for shipments in their possession with notably few exceptions. The development of English common law was for the protection of the shipper almost exclusively. And a carrier's only defense is that the damage or loss is attributable to an act of God or the public enemy. Today the motor common carrier of general commodities in the United States has much the same liability for goods as early-day carriers, in that the firm is for the most part almost absolutely liable. Of over 10,000 items in the National Motor Freight Classification 100-C, only 33 presently provide for released values limiting carrier liability. Technology may have overtaken the concepts of common law liability as presently established, and today's goods are not comparable to yesteryear's consignments, as a wider range of values exists today.

FIGURE 1

Total 1971 Traffic
(average operating ratio = 94.6 percent)

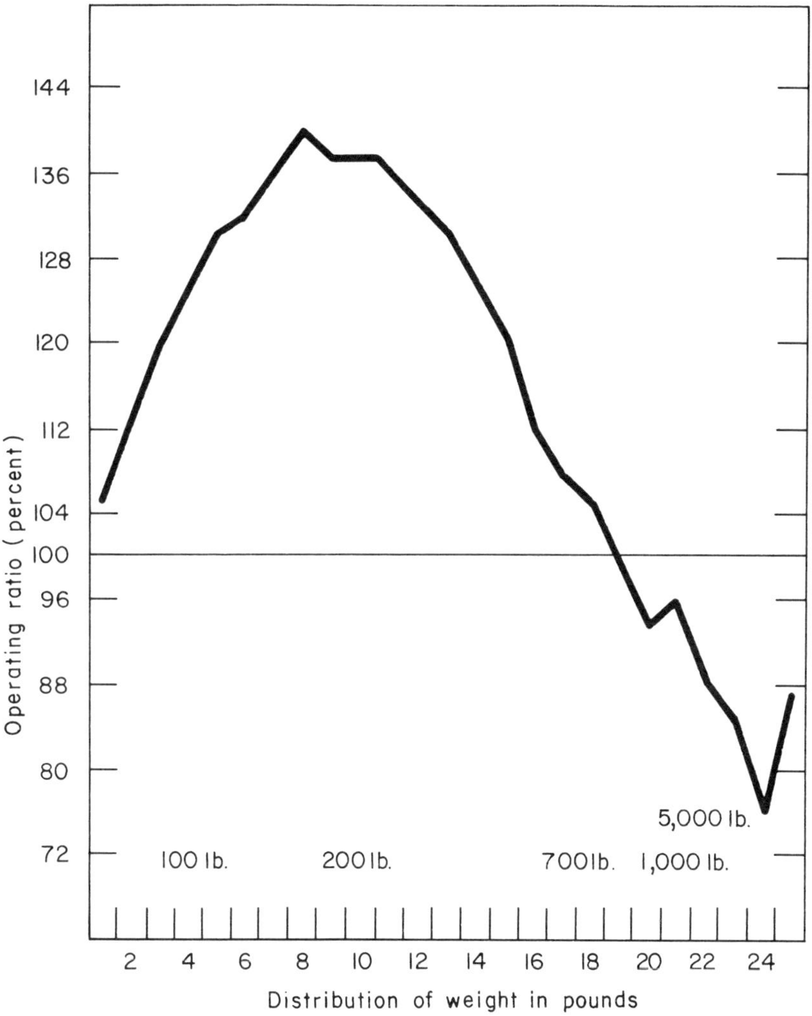

Note: Each cell represents 1/25 or 4 percent of total shipments. Ratios are worse than 100 (on the average) all the way up to shipments of nearly 700 lbs.

Source: American Trucking Association, Inc., 1971, Cost/ Revenue Analysis.

The common carrier system in early England is not comparable with the modern-day motor common carrier in the United States. Presently, the United States has a network of structured business firms operating tractors and trailers over superhighways. In early England a carrier might be in business today and completely disappear from the scene tomorrow. There is a continuity in today's structured firm, and this continuity is to a great extent reliant on sustained carrier performance. A favorable experience in the cargo loss and damage area is beyond doubt an impetus toward continuity of a common carrier firm. Survival of the trucking firm cannot rely solely on new business every day. There is only service to sell, and if service declines, revenue declines. Common carriers, of course, must continue to be liable for goods in their care, and the ICC is empowered by Congress to enforce this legal concept.

Shippers must have a means of protecting goods in transit. The questions are, what party should shoulder the responsibility and what is the magnitude of liability? Historically, the common carrier system has assumed all of the responsibility for cargo loss and damage to goods in its possession with a few exceptions in the form of released rates orders. Motor common carriers of general commodities are insurers of goods without the privilege of knowing their attendant risk, as shippers are not normally required to disclose the value of a shipment.

One important public policy implication of this is that it would appear reasonable if limits or liability could be discreetly established. Such a move may be imperative to the preservation of a strong and viable national transportation system. Possible inequities in the rate structure between the small and large shipments might also be eliminated through such a limitation of liability and a simplified rating plan.

Presently the ICC appears to have assumed the posture associated with a willingness to listen to the problems of the motor carriers. The attitude of the courts and regulatory agencies toward motor carrier liability has in the past been static. On the other hand, other modes of transportation have been granted simplified rate structures with the shifting of liability for cargo loss and damage through released rates or ratings. A new approach to carrier liability in the motor carrier industry could result in lower freight costs to the shipping public.[3]

METHODOLOGY

The primary purpose for this research effort is threefold: evaluating common carrier liability as applicable to motor common carriers of general commodities; providing insight into cargo loss and damage expense and the potential for cost savings to the motor carrier through a reduction of this expense on small shipments; and attempting to develop a mathematical model for the purpose of predicting cargo loss and damage probability and amount.

There are two principal approaches to solving the small shipment problem: reduce the cost of handling the small shipment or increase the revenue earned on small shipments. Excessive increases in revenue might prevent some freight from moving, a possibility not conducive to a wide distribution of manufactured goods throughout the nation. If the small shipment could be made profitable at approximately the same revenue, and a reasonable profit margin maintained on larger shipments, the motor carrier industry could continue to exercise its inherent advantage of speed and flexibility.

This book will emphasize two cost-saving techniques affiliated with cargo loss and damage and common carrier liability. These two techniques have been combined in various proposals for small shipment rate restructuring. The dual thrust of these proposals focuses upon cost reduction through a simplified rating plan and a simultaneous limitation of carrier liability. Cost may be diminished in both areas and in addition such a plan may be considerably less discriminatory in that prices will be basically cost-oriented rather than value-of-service-oriented.

The small shipment restructuring proposals presented by the Middle Atlantic Conference, for instance, would have the effect of reducing the number of classification ratings to a minimum and would limit carrier liability for such shipments to a maximum value as declared by the shipper.[4] In reality, the small shipment is a unique commodity, a commodity that meets the criteria stipulated by the ICC for the approval of released rates.[5]

One pertinent question is: would carrier cost savings made possible through the shifting of liability for cargo loss and damage claims and through the savings in indirect operating cost result in a net decrease in transportation cost in the total economy? Apparently, the total cost savings could be substantial if some sort of released rating plan were initiated for small shipments. Indirect costs, such as claims inspection process, claims department personnel costs, and billing costs, could be reduced. If claims experience remained relatively constant on an aggregate basis after the new plan was instigated, the savings in the indirect cost of billing shipments could be a real gain to the economy. This gain would most likely appear in the form of relatively lower shipping costs on larger shipments. Subsidization of the small shipment by larger shipments would be reduced or eliminated and a net economic cost reduction achieved. Only if the claims experience increased could such a plan be considered uneconomical.

This research effort is expected to answer the following major questions considered to be important for rate restructuring proposals.

1. What percentage of shipments of the study carrier has a computed value per pound of less than $3, $4, or $5?
2. What are the claims ratios experienced by the study carrier in the following weight brackets: minimum charge, 1 to 199 pounds, 200 to 499 pounds, 500 to 999 pounds, 1,000 to 1,999 pounds, 2,000 to 4,999 pounds, 5,000 to 9,999 pounds, 10,000 and over, total LTL, total minimum charge and LTL, truckload, total all shipments?
3. If shipments weighing less than 1,000 pounds had been released at values not to exceed $3 per pound, $4 per pound, or $5 per pound, what would be the dollar cost claims savings that could conceivably be utilized in restructuring for more equitable rates?
4. What transportation variables are the best discriminators between shipments that result in paid claims and those shipments on which no claims have been paid?
5. Can a model be constructed using the variables in question 4 that will provide the probability that a shipment will fall into that group of shipments that is susceptible to loss or damage? May the model be used as a predictor of the probability of cargo loss and damage to individual shipments?
6. Can a multiple regression model be constructed using the above variables to predict the amount of cargo loss and damage expense of a motor carrier?

The necessary data for this work were collected from a motor truck common carrier of general commodities. The principal objective was to provide insight into cargo loss and damage expense of the motor carrier, and, for this purpose, a number of tables are prepared for examination. They include frequency distributions of shipment value per pound in $1 per pound increments, claims ratios by weight brackets, dollar claims cost savings from released valuation limits, and claims cost savings by commodity groups. The purpose for compiling these tables was to differentiate claims cost experience between large and small shipments and among respective commodity groups. An analysis of information contained in these tables provides a relationship between cargo loss and damage and small shipments for use in rate restructuring proposals.

Discriminant analysis is employed for the purpose of isolating those transportation variables that are the best discriminators between claims shipments and no-claims shipments. This procedure has been used with various financial ratios as variables in predicting good and bad bank loans and isolating those ratios that are the best discriminators between the two groups. A definition of multiple discriminant analysis is given by Edward Altman:

> MDA is a statistical technique used to classify an observation into one of several a priori groupings dependent upon the observation's individual characteristics. It is used primarily to classify and/or make predictions in problems where the independent variable appears in qualitative form, e.g., male or female, bankrupt or non-bankrupt.[6]

The statistical package for the social sciences subprogram discriminant is utilized in the study to locate those variables that contribute most to a separation of the no-claims group and the claims group of shipments.[7] Classification functions are derived for each of the two groups for the purpose of classifying shipments as either claims or no-claims on the basis of the discriminating variable.

Discriminant analysis will not categorically determine that a shipment will result in a claim or not result in a claim. But the model reflects that a shipment has claims symptoms, as measured by transportation variables, similar to those other shipments that have resulted in paid claims.

The prediction ability of the discriminant model is tested against the prior probabilities of correct classification inherent in the sample data as well as against the prior probabilities of a claim occurrence as provided by carrier records. Discriminant analysis assigns a shipment to one of the designated groups but cannot predict the amount of cargo loss and damage expense. The model for predicting cargo loss and damage expense for the motor carrier is developed employing the statistical package for the social science subprogram regression.[8] The variables to be used in the multiple regression will be the monthly aggregates of those determined by the discriminant analysis to be the best discriminators between the no-claims and the claims groups of shipments.

To test the overall goodness of fit of the regression model, the null hypothesis is tested that the multiple correlation in the model is zero, or,

$$H_o: R = 0$$

$$H_1: R \neq 0$$

Additional tests of the individual regression coefficients are made using a hierarchical procedure. The null hypothesis is such that variables X_3, X_4 . . . do not add significantly to the variation in Y, already explained by X_1 and X_2, etc.

The investigation was limited to one motor truck common carrier of general commodities. (This carrier, however, is representative of most large general commodity motor carriers in terms of traffic composition, values, revenues, and claims.) Operations of this carrier cover a large geographical area, most of the region east of the Mississippi River and a sizable area immediately west of the Mississippi River. However, more conclusive results with reference to value per pound and claims ratio studies should be obtainable from a broad cross-sectional study of motor carriers. Shipments occurring within only 18 months were included in the sample. Better results should be obtained from a five-year study with two or three years' data available for testing.

NOTES

1. Title 49 USC. For an in-depth probe of the U.S. national transportation policy, see Grant M. Davis and Jack J. Holder, Jr., "Does the U.S. Have a Cohesive National Transportation Policy?" ICC Practitioners' Journal 41, no. 3 (March-April 1974):332-49.

2. In this regard the ICC will no doubt do a great deal of study before allowing the removal of restrictions on daily weight such as proposed by United Parcel Service. See "UPS Asks ICC for Relief from Certain Weight Restrictions," Traffic World, November 29, 1976, p. 55.

3. Interstate Commerce Commission, Ex Parte No. MC-98, New Procedures in Motor Carrier Restructuring Proceedings, Notice of Proposed Rule Making (Washington, D.C., 1975), p. 1. Also consult "O'Neal Examines Problems with Released Rates, Calls for Further Study," Traffic World 173, no. 2 (January 1978):23.

4. Middle Atlantic Conference, Released Rates Application Seeking Released Valuation Rate for Application on All Commodity Rates and Charges on Shipments Weighing Less Than 1,000 Pounds, 1975.

5. Interstate Commerce Commission, Released Rates Order No. MC-920, Denying Released Rates Application No. MC-1408, All Shipments Weighing Less Than 300 Pounds (May 1976).

6. Edward I. Altman, "Financial Ratios, Discriminant Analysis and the Prediction of Corporate Bankruptcy," Journal of Finance 23 (September 1968):591.

7. Norman H. Nie et al., eds., Statistical Package for the Social Sciences (New York: McGraw-Hill, 1975), p. 434.

8. Ibid., p. 320.

2

HISTORY OF THE SMALL SHIPMENT PROBLEM

The long-range goal of management may vary with companies; however, the overall minimum corporate goal is survival. To survive, the firm must earn sufficient profits from operations to provide a fair return on assets employed in the venture, in addition to providing funds for dividends and reinvestment in the business. The resulting earnings should be sufficiently favorable to attract new investment capital for expansion and to replace depreciated plant and equipment. This problem is not only the responsibility of management but is of utmost importance to the regulatory agencies concerned with transportation. Joint problems faced by both regulatory agencies and carrier management include pricing transportation service, regulatory lag, and the improvement of cost information for management and regulatory decision making.

The Interstate Commerce Commission implements and controls rate regulation for interstate motor carriers of freight and passengers. This regulatory agency is confronted with the complex problems of protecting both industry and the national interest. Among the uses for which cost information is of importance to the ICC are to determine if rates are compensatory, to determine if they are excessive, to determine if they are unduly prejudiced, to ascertain the most economical mode of transportation, and to determine fairness of division of joint rates.[1]

In order to accomplish these goals, the ICC should expect, demand, and, furthermore, create realistic cost measures for transport pricing purposes.[2] Application of the rule of rate making followed by the ICC is contained in Title 49 of the USC:

> In the exercise of its power to prescribe just and reasonable rates the Commission shall give due consideration to many other factors, to the effect of rates on the movement of traffic . . . and to the need of revenue sufficient to enable the carriers under honest, economical, and efficient management to provide such service.

> The ultimate objective of the existing body of regulatory law is to develop, coordinate and preserve a national transportation system under private ownership and operation capable of meeting the expanding needs of commerce of the country, the postal service and national defense, with the general burden of expense or cost necessary to support such a system fairly and reasonably apportioned among the users of the services.[3]

As John Creedy remarks, "Prices are severely regulated in transportation, the utilities, and communications but their costs are totally unregulated."[4] Freight rates have been compared with cost controls controlling inflation, in that freight rates lag far behind the consumer and wholesale price indexes. Rates never do catch up with "massive cost increases" and the transport industry is forced into a cost rate spiral with no opportunity to escape.

The case load of the ICC and state regulatory agencies represents a time-consuming, expensive process for determining whether rates are compensatory, fair, and reasonable and meet the requirements for intermodal competition as delineated by the commission.[5] According to Roy Sampson and Martin Farris, during a recent year 7,346 formal proceedings were reviewed by the commission, and these formal cases were in addition to many informal complaints. Cases are frequently carried forward into following years.[6]

The present regulatory process may deprive the carriers and the public of resources for investment in at least three fundamental ways: the inevitable regulatory lag, the underdepreciation problem, and the problem of profitability. Creedy points out that during the time allowed for questions and answers to objections in rate cases, hundreds of millions of justifiable revenues are forgone.[7]

The formal hearing and its adversary format and the reliance on due process are both time consuming and costly. What is needed are ways in which rate cases may be resolved in a realistic and expeditious manner with a stable, long-term approach.[8]

This book delves into a major current problem for the motor common carrier industry and the users of its service. The tendrils of the cargo loss and damage problem and associated common carrier liability are inextricably intermingled with the problems of profitability and regulatory lag. According to one study conducted in 1972 almost $1 of every $50 received by motor carriers was paid out in cargo loss and damage claims. The respondents in this study numbered 366 and average annual sales for a responding firm was $25 million; the range of sales varied from $100,000 to multimillion-dollar concerns. Seventy-five percent of the firms ranked trucking as their most important method of shipment.[9] The total cost of loss and damage for the group was $31,247,177, and trucking was designated as the carrier involved in about 50 percent of this. About 7 percent of the total loss and damage claims for 1970 were represented by the study group.[10]

An examination of the Quarterly Freight Loss and Damage Claim report prepared by the ICC for the quarter ended September 30, 1975, indicates that common carriers of general freight expended $36,922,818 as a result of 462,266 claims paid. Recoveries from salvage amounted to $4,955,919 and from insurance $938,604, for a net outlay of dollars in payment of claims of $31,028,295. The ratio of net claims paid to net revenue during the quarter was 1.03 percent.[11] This claims ratio is, of course, an average. Commodities that are highly susceptible to cargo loss or damage will reflect a much higher claims ratio. For instance, another study compiled by the National Freight Claims Council revealed a claims ratio for reporting carriers of 1.70 percent for all commodities. The corresponding ratio for clothing was 5.09 percent.[12]

The costs of cargo loss and damage claims to the individual carrier are not all reflected in claims ratios. Other costs to be included would be the indirect cost of handling and paying claims, that is, claims inspection process, claims department management and clerical personnel, as well as computer time used in processing and controlling claims. Depreciation on office equipment and building space used by the claims department should also be considered as cargo loss and damage expense by the carrier. Motor carriers have indicated that their indirect costs vary from $2 to $5 in processing claims, paperwork, and manpower for every dollar of direct cost.[13] These figures were published in 1971 and, of course, would be considerably higher due to inflationary influences.

> Published statistics indicate that at least two-thirds of the loss and damage to shipper goods may be controllable. That is, about one-third may be attributable to rough handling by carriers either at terminals or en route. Another one-third may be due to improper packaging, marking, or loading by the shipper. The remainder is the result of unknown or uncontrollable factors.[14]

"At least 15 cents of every 36 to 39 cents motor carriers are paying for visible freight damage is being paid for damage that is not the carrier's fault," according to a three-and-one-half-year study by the Shock and Vibration Subcommittee of the National Freight Claim Council's Freight Loss and Damage Prevention Committee.[15] It is the result of shock and vibration, which is not under a carrier's control—a variable that no shipper can afford to package because so many variables are involved.[16]

According to the National Freight Claim Council's Freight Loss and Damage Prevention Committee, mathematical projection indicates that every truck engaged in hauling freight is subject to the occurrence of "resonant frequency." This phenomenon can affect some portion of a cargo regardless of the precaution taken by the carrier or shipper. Apparently this phenomenon is an uncontrollable element ever present in the highway transportation of freight. "A series of small shocks or a constant uniform movement can cause damage." The catalyst is the matching of the frequency caused by movement of the vehicle with the natural frequency of movement of individual items in the load. When these match, "resonance" results and produces damage.[17]

Statistics compiled by the U.S. Department of Transportation indicate that the bulk of crime loss is at terminals rather than when goods are en route. "Pilferage predominates the crime loss and usually the crime is committed by carrier employees who are authorized to be on the premises." Items most often stolen include clothing, electrical appliances, automotive parts, food products, hardware, jewelry, tobacco products, scientific instruments, and alcoholic beverages.[18]

The group on which A. H. McKinley reported ranked improper handling outside the vehicle as the number one cause of damage. This was subsequently followed by improper loading of the linehaul vehicle and severe shock and vibration en route as causes two and three, respectively. This particular study also revealed that 30 percent of damage was of the concealed variety,[19] or damage to freight discovered after delivery of the shipment to the consignee in apparent good order without previous evidence of irregularity.[20] Of the study group, 44 percent maintained statistics on loss and damage claims.

Small shipments do require more platform handling than larger shipments. In other words, the probability is greater that a small shipment will be handled more at origin, intermediate, and destination points.[21] It follows that the more times a shipment is handled, the more susceptible it is to loss or damage.

From the point of view of the shipper, a large volume of claims indicates that a firm is not providing proper service as a common carrier.[22] This viewpoint may be caused by a lack of security measures by the carrier to prevent theft and pilferage or lack of proper employee training programs oriented toward the prevention of loss and damage. A high claims experience could also be related to product characteristics or failure of the shipper to take all precautions necessary to protect goods from loss or damage.

No individual or firm benefits from lost and damaged shipments. "Lost and damaged shipments are a sheer loss to the nation's economy, resulting both in lost production and higher freight rates and higher consumer prices."[23] All members of the channel of distribution are inconvenienced by damaged and lost merchandise. Production schedules are disrupted and there is a deterioration of goodwill among the carrier, shipper, and consignee.[24] "The breakdown in physical distribution performance from loss and damage claims constitutes a deficiency to the shipper firm in the eyes of customers."[25] Even the satisfactory adjustment of loss and damage claims is a poor substitute for the arrival of a shipment in good condition."[26]

"To effect claim prevention periodic analysis must be made of claim records to detect the causes."[27] By determining the causes, remedial steps can be initiated to minimize the causative factors and thereby improve the service rendered to the customer. Claims improvement will not occur unless both carriers and shippers are cognizant that cargo loss and damage increase both carrier and shipper costs.[28] In addition to necessary higher rates, distribution systems are affected by cargo loss and damage through the erosion of service levels caused by reduced inventory. Neither the shipper, carrier, nor consignee benefits when a loss and damage claim occurs.

Unless a common motor carrier's liability is mitigated through one of only a few provisions contained in either the bill of lading or through tariff provisions approved by the ICC, the firm is liable to the owner of the goods for its full actual loss resulting from any damage to or loss of all or part of a shipment. Common carrier liability may be limited in some instances because of fault of the shipper, the inherent nature of the goods, or refusal to handle goods of extraordinary value. Legal reduction of liability for the transport of any given commodity may be obtained through ICC approval of released value rates for that commodity. But carrier applications for released rates are seldom approved.

Motor carriers have made a number of applications for released value rates or ratings on all or various commodities throughout the years, but, the commission has approved the proposals in only a few instances. In December 1975, over 10,000 items were included in the National Motor Freight Classification 100-B, but only 33 items were subject to released rates.[29] Thus, only about .33 percent of all commodities are covered by released rates. The commission has applied the power to approve released value rates or ratings sparingly. Among the denied applications were proposals for released value rates on clothing and data processing equipment.[30]

In 1955, an effort was initiated to publish a general classification rule that would limit liability to $3 per pound or $150 per package, whichever was greater, or $100,000 per shipment unless a greater value was declared by the shipper with appropriate higher charges.[31] Numerous attempts to limit carrier liability have been denied because the commission has not been persuaded that sufficient proof was presented to establish the criteria necessary for released value rates or ratings. Released Rates Order MC-917, a request for released rates on commodities requiring special handling or the use of special equipment and related contractor materials, supplies, and equipment, was denied. The board concluded insufficient evidence was presented, as no high ratio of claims to the number of shipments was conclusively demonstrated.[32]

The purpose of this chapter is to provide a review of the literature for a background of the rate structure problem.

CARRIER LIABILITY FOR CARGO LOSS AND DAMAGE

All carriers strive to give service to shippers that will meet the shippers' need and ensure that the goods arrive in satisfactory condition. Furthermore, section 20(11) of the Interstate Commerce Act stipulates that a carrier is absolutely liable for all loss, damage, or injury to goods transported by it with only a few exceptions.[33] Despite the many technological advances made in preventing or reducing damage to shipments, "the human element still remains a source of accidents."[34] Even motor carriers with claims ratios well below the national average reach a point below which the ratio cannot fall.

"The liability of a common carrier commences on delivery of the goods to it for transportation, that is, as soon as the delivery is complete and the possession of the goods has been transferred from the shipper to the carrier."[35] Also, the liability associated with the common carrier is almost unlimited in nature and the firm may limit this liability in very few ways. The common carrier's duty is to deliver the goods entrusted to its care.[36]

"Common carriers are responsible for loss, damage, or delay to freight while in their possession and this liability is based on (1) common law, (2) statutory law, (3) lawful conditions of the contract of shipment (bill of lading), and (4) pertinent provisions of applicable tariffs on file with the Interstate Commerce Commission as to interstate transportation."[37] Liability is strict and the carrier has few statutory defenses. Statutory and case law have established a legal framework that provides little relief for the carrier and its responsibility for goods.

Negligence of the carrier when goods are lost or damaged is usually presumed. In fact, Richard Sigmon states: "The liability of a common carrier is not predicated on negligence or fault, since he is held liable to the shipper or owner of the goods for all losses or injuries to freight in his possession, without regard for the question of negligence except those losses or injuries resulting from five narrowly defined causes."[38] In the United States the common carrier cannot limit liability merely by direct notice to the shipper or by a general notice to the public.[39] The owner "it is said" has the right to insist that the carrier accept and carry the goods subject to all incidents of its employment.[40] The only way to a limitation of liability by the carrier is through a petition to the ICC for approval of released or stated value rates.

Section 20, paragraph 11, of part E of the Interstate Commerce Act provides that in the event of loss, damage, or injury to freight the carrier issuing the bill of lading or receipt shall be liable to the lawful holder of the bill of lading or receipt or to any party entitled to recover thereon, for the "full actual loss, damage or injury to such property caused by it or any common carrier."[41]

> The courts have generally recognized that (1) the shipper, (b) the consignee, (3) the owner of the goods, (d) the insurance company as a subrogee, or (e) the holder of a straight bill of lading, even though at the time the action is brought is no longer the owner of the goods damaged, may file suit against a carrier for loss or damage to goods while in transit.[42]

The damaged shipper or consignee or other party "may file claim with either the delivering carrier or the originating carrier."[43]

When a loss or damage claim is being settled both shipper and carrier naturally pursue their own interests, and their separate assessments of the loss may be highly divergent; however, "Under the provisions of the law . . . , the question of damages is usually one of fact—<u>what was the actual loss of the claimant</u>? . . . the law is concerned with restoration of the claimant to the same position he would have occupied had there been no loss and damage" [Emphasis added].[44] Under this interpretation, the claimant shipper or consignee would be entitled usually to the invoice price of goods less any applicable trade discounts and the freight charges on the lost and damaged shipment, if paid. Normally, the claimant's profit is not a liability of the carrier unless it is shown that such profit had been earned through a prior sale.

The evolvement of early common law is reflected in the present law of loss and damage claims. The U.S. statutory law is closely related to the common law, and when one considers them together, there has been little change in carrier liability through the years. According to Thomas Skulina, the rules pertaining to intrastate and interstate movements are well settled once the evidence of the case justifies identifying the movement as solely within one state or that between two or more states.[45]

Common Law Liability

In common law the implied agreement of common carriers is to carry safely, and they are strictly accountable for the loss of and failure to deliver goods received by them for carriage.[46] In 1703, Lord Holt, in the famous English case Coggs v. Bernard stated the common law liability of carriers as "he is bound to answer for the goods in all events."[47]

> The law charges this person thus entrusted to carry goods, against all events, but acts of God and of enemies of the King. For though the force be ever so great, as if an irresistible multitude of people should rob him, nevertheless he is chargeable.[48]

Lord Holt's decision provided a number of rules establishing varying degrees of liability "or standards of care" applicable to different types of bailments. The carrier for hire, according to Holt, is chargeable with the highest degree of care.[49] "He is liable for all loss or damage which may happen to goods while in his charge for purposes of transportation, though occasioned by unavoidable accident, or by any casualty whatever, except for an act of God or of a public enemy."[50] Lord Holt described an act of God as an act as could not happen by the intervention of man, such as storms, lightning, or tempests.[51] An act of the public enemy is defined as an act by armed forces of an enemy nation.[52]

If the damage or loss is for reason of act of God or the public enemy, the carrier could not be presumed to have control of means to prevent the loss or damage. A court of law may not find for the shipper in claim cases when the damage was caused by one of these reasons. Some events that have been held to be acts of God are "floods of extraordinary character, wind or rainstorm of unusual violence and snow storms blocking the right of way." The public enemy does not include hoodlums; it is associated with foreign military forces of an enemy nation.[53]

While older theory equated an act of God with an inevitable or unavoidable accident, now the interpretation characterizes such an event as caused by natural forces rather than the consequence of any human agency.[54] The liability now assumed by the common carrier includes liability for loss and damage from all causes with the following exceptions: an act of God, the public enemy, the authority of law, the act or default of the shipper, and natural shrinkage or inherent nature or vice of the goods.[55]

When the loss is not due to one of these excepted causes, it is immaterial whether or not the carrier is negligent. When the damage to a shipment is for a reason other than one of those enumerated above, the carrier is absolutely liable for the full value of the loss except when the commodity is covered by released rates.[56] Strict liability has continued to be the basic law with respect to common carriers within the United States.[57] Even if there is a loss of or damage to goods in the possession of the carrier due to one of these exclusions in the bill of lading contract, "the carrier might be liable if it could be shown that it failed to use reasonable care either to avoid the peril or to minimize the loss or damage after the goods were actually exposed to the peril.[58]

The common law rule is based on a number of considerations including the public character of the carrier's duties, the inequality in the footing of the carrier and the shipper, the absolute possession and control of the property, and the entire separation of the property from the shipper in the course of transportation.[59] The vulnerability of the shipper, then, is the ethic behind common law carrier liability. A basic question arises regarding the means of accomplishing the protection of this shipper vulnerability and whether or not it is in harmony with the protection achieved.

Another question is whether or not present-day economic goals are best served by the application of strict liability in the historic common law sense. The risks involved in handling shipments by the common carrier are great and vary among the different commodities flowing through the transportation system. One purpose of economic regulation is the prevention of discrimination. Technological progress has presented the world with grand new innovations in electronics, chemistry, and atomic energy. The present-day combination of man's efforts and materials may result in unit values of products that have no comparable counterpart in history. Is the value of space age vehicle parts and the liability therefor comparable to values of parts for horse-drawn carriages and the liability therefor? These are questions to which the answers are important. If space age products are not comparable to products for which the common law was developed, what changes, then, should be made to best provide for the allocation of transportation resources without discrimination?

The need for federal regulation in the transportation industry is readily apparent, especially from the point of view of loss and damage claims. Different rules of law in different states would be quite unwieldy in the settlement of any claim for loss or damage to shipments moving through two or more states or moving coast to coast.[60]

Act to Regulate Commerce and the Hepburn Act

The monopoly of transportation by the railroads necessitated the passage of some sort of legislation for control in order to protect the public. The Interstate Commerce Act of 1887 was therefore enacted by Congress. The provisions of the act were inadequate in reference to public protection in the form of requirements for assumption of liability for shipments by the railroads who "continued" to issue bills of lading with liability limiting clauses.[61] "Inherent in the rationale behind the Interstate Commerce Act is its designed purpose to promote harmonious interstate transportation and thereby aid commerce and avoid discrimination."[62]

The Hepburn Act of 1906 contained what is commonly called the Carmack Amendment.[63] "The purpose of the Carmack Amendment was two-fold—to completely regulate commerce, and to hold the initial carrier liable for loss, damage or injury caused by it or a connecting carrier."[64] The initial carrier did have the privilege of collecting from the connecting line.[65] The act provided that no contract, receipt, rule or regulation could exempt the originating carrier from full liability.[66] As far as loss and damage claims are concerned, the Carmack Amendment also had the effect of federalizing the states' regulatory authority. Property shipped in interstate commerce was placed under federal regulation.[67] The primary modification of common law brought about by the passage of the Carmack Amendment is that "a prima facie case of negligence is established when it is proven that the shipment was received at the point of origin in good condition and was received in a damaged state at the point of destination."[68]

The Carmack Amendment has been interpreted as providing liability for the carrier for loss and damage incurred because of negligence but not limiting or prohibiting agreements to reduce liability or a reduction of liability through regulation.[69] Confusion existed concerning the requirements of the act with reference to the carrier's right to limit its liability through special contractual arrangements and "limiting clauses" continued to appear in bills of lading.[70] The court attempted to clarify this problem in Adams Express v. Croninger in 1913, holding that by reasonable and just agreement the common law liability could be mitigated through the medium of an agreed reduced value for the shipment noted on the bill of lading or express receipt.[71]

The Cummins Amendments

After the Adams Express Company v. Croninger case, the Coggs v. Bernard limitation relative to full carrier liability was discarded for a return to the proposition that carriers could limit their liability by making a "special acceptance."[72] The situation was so confused after the Adams v. Croninger decision that some carriers varied their claims payments and sometimes ignored the fact that lost or damaged shipments moved at released rates and paid full value. This, of course, led to charges of discrimination.[73]

Because of the plethora of disagreements relative to released valuation in bills of lading, Congress passed the first Cummins Amendment in 1915.[74] This amendment made the carrier liable for the full actual loss, damage, or injury to property entrusted to it and no agreement as to value was permitted on any document. There was no mitigation of liability through rate reduction or agreements according to most interpretations.[75] There was provision, however, that if goods were hidden from view, the shipper could be required to declare the value of the goods in writing. The ICC was empowered to establish rates for these shipments. The amendment also extended the Carmack Amendment to cover adjacent foreign countries.[76] "In 1916 Congress passed the Second Cummins Amendment to provide that carriers might lawfully limit their liability by released rates that had been specifically approved by the Interstate Commerce Commission."[77]

This restored the system of released rates that was declared unlawful by the first Cummins Amendment. The decision as to when released rates would be just and reasonable was left to the jurisdiction of the ICC, and the agency's approval was required by the act before released rates could be applied. The present provisions of section 20(11) of the Interstate Commerce Act are a reflection of the second Cummins Amendment.[78]

Interstate Commerce Act Section 20(11)

The provisions of the Carmack Amendment to the Hepburn Act of 1906 as amended by the two Cummins amendments are much like the present provisions of section 20(11).[79] The act provided for the liability of a common carrier when transporting goods in interstate commerce. The liability is extensive and empowers the ICC to establish rates for goods shipped under released valuation. This section and section 20(12) of the act are applicable to motor carriers in 49 USC Section 319. Section 20(11) is reproduced in part:

> Any common carrier, railroad, or transportation company subject to the provisions of this chapter receiving property for transportation from a point in one state . . . to a point in another state . . . shall issue a receipt or a bill of lading to the lawful holder thereof for any loss,

damage or injury to such property caused by it or any common carrier, railroad or transportation company to which such property may be delivered or over whose line or lines such property may pass within the United States or within an adjacent foreign country when transported on a through bill of lading, and no contract, receipt, rule, regulation or other limitation of any character whatsoever shall exempt such common carrier, railroad or transportation company from the liability hereby imposed; and any such common carrier . . . so receiving property for transportation . . . or any common carrier delivering said property so received and transported shall be liable . . . for the full actual loss, damage, or injury to such property caused by it or any such common carrier, . . . to which said property may be delivered or over whose line or lines such property may pass . . . notwithstanding any limitation of the amount of recovery or representation or agreement as to value in any . . . receipt or bill of lading or in any contract, rule, regulation or in any tariff filed with the Interstate Commerce Commission; and any such limitation, . . . is declared to be unlawful and void: Provided that (limitation of liability to that of water carriers) Provided, however, that the provisions hereof respecting liability for full loss, damage or injury . . . shall not apply, . . . to property except ordinary livestock, received for transportation concerning which the carrier shall have been or shall be expressly authorized or required by order of the Interstate Commerce Commission to establish and maintain rates dependent upon the value declared in writing by the shipper or agreed upon in writing as the released value of the property in which case the agreement will have no other effect than to limit liability and recovery to an amount not exceeding the value so declared or released, and shall not, so far as relates to values, be held to be in violation of section 10 of this title; and any tariff schedule which may be filed with the Commission pursuant to such order shall contain specific reference thereto and may establish rates varying with the value so declared and agreed upon; and the Commission is empowered to make such order where rates dependent upon and varying with declared or agreed values would, in its opinion, be just and reasonable under the circumstances and

> conditions surrounding the transportation.[80] [emphasis added]

The Motor Carrier Act of 1935 provided federal regulation of motor carrier highway transportation, and this is now part II of the Interstate Commerce Act. No new provisions were made to govern motor carrier liability for goods transported. The liability imposed upon railroads was made applicable to motor carriers also by section 219 (49 USC 219) as follows: "The provisions of section 20(11) of Part I shall apply with like force and effect to receipts or bills of lading of common carriers by motor vehicles."[81]

The Bill of Lading

Kenneth Flood notes that while many believe the carrier to be absolutely liable for goods in its possession, this is not the case because of the limitation provision on the bill of lading.[82] In the United States, the bill of lading is a form of agreement, a contract, between the carrier and the shipper that has the effect of limiting the carrier's liability. There has been no formal prescription of a uniform bill of lading for the motor carrier industry, though the Motor Carrier Act of 1935 provided that the motor carrier must issue a receipt or bill of lading for any property picked up for transportation. In 1946 the ICC ordered that certain information be included in the bill of receipt, such as the names of consignor and consignee and the points of origin or destination.[83] The bill of lading serves as a receipt for goods, certifies that the goods shown thereon were received in apparent good order, and were properly marked. In some cases it serves as evidence of title to goods.[84] The contract further provides that the carrier's liability is that of a warehouseman should the carrier attempt to deliver goods to the shipper and because of an act of shipper is unable to complete delivery.[85]

Section 1(b) of the terms of the Uniform Domestic Bill of Lading provides that a carrier's liability is that of a warehouseman "for loss, damage or delay from fire occurring after the expiration of the time allowed in the carrier's tariff." Care to property provided by a warehouseman is that care an "ordinary prudent person" would provide for his own property under similar circumstances.[86] The bill of lading also serves as notice to the shipper that goods shown thereon move under the rules of tariffs on file with the ICC.

The exemptions from common law liability shown on the bill of lading are related directly to the five narrowly defined areas discussed in the previous section. These provide that the carrier is not liable at common law for loss or damage caused by acts of God, acts or default of the shipper, act of the public enemy, inherent nature of the goods, or acts of government or public authority. Such phrases as "shipped at owner's risk" or "carrier not responsible for faulty packing" on the bill of lading have no effect in limiting carrier liability.[87]

Flood distinguishes bill of lading liability and common law liability. Under his interpretation, common law liability is such that the carrier is subject to liability for all loss and damage to goods handled by it, for all causes, other than acts of God or public enemy. The other exclusions relate to bill of lading liability. The shipper may elect to receive the increased common law coverage of the shipment for the risk of cargo loss or damage by making proper notation on the bill of lading and paying 10 percent freight charges in addition to the normal class rate. Shippers seldom request that carriers assume this increased liability.[88]

Section 2 of the Federal Bill of Lading Act provides that the carrier is not required to transport property by any manner other than that necessitated by reasonable dispatch. The carrier's own schedule of normal operations would be governing in determining reasonable dispatch. Should the carrier take longer than its schedule, "the claimant will usually establish a prima facie case that the carrier has breached its duty to transport with reasonable dispatch."[89] In such situations, it is the carrier's burden to "explain the delay by showing it was not due to negligence on his part" but was due to causes beyond his control.[90]

The general rule is that it is the carrier's burden of proof to establish that any loss or damage to a shipment is within the narrowly defined exclusions printed on the bill of lading. Richard Sigmon notes that the general rule held by the Supreme Court is that the burden of proof is on the carrier to prove that any loss or damage applicable to a shipment is attributable to one of the exceptions printed on the bill of lading. In the case of perishable articles, for example, Sigmon notes that a number of lower court decisions have held that the carrier must only show its compliance with tariff rules and any shipper instructions but that the Supreme Court places the burden of proof on the carrier.[91]

"The rights and liabilities of parties to an interstate shipment depend upon Acts of Congress, the bill of lading terms, and common law principles."[92] Tariffs, when lawfully on file with the ICC, have the force and effect of a federal statute. Therefore, provisions in applicable classification and freight tariffs also govern carrier liability.[93]

A general proposition exists that a common carrier may by contract limit its liability, except for damages or loss resulting from negligence of the carrier or its agents or servants.[94] Such statements are the rule in the absence of constitutional or statutory provisions against liability limitation. In regard to this general proposition, John Miller notes: "The law is now well settled that a carrier may, when not forbidden by statute, limit or restrict or even extend and enlarge, its common-law liability. . . . In view of statutory provisions today, however, the right is practically meaningless."[95]

Limitations of Liability[96]

> Limitations of carrier liability at common law include acts of God and acts of public enemy. In addition, limitations have been added by statute and these include acts of public authority, acts of the shipper, and the inherent nature of the goods. Whenever loss or damage happens to goods for reason other than these common law and bill of lading exemptions, the shipper has a right of recovery against the carrier for his full actual loss or for the agreed value of the goods if the shipment moves under released valuation rules and rates as established by the Interstate Commerce Commission. Under Section 20 as amended any attempted limitation of the shipper's right of recovery for the full actual loss, damage, or injury to property received for transportation is declared to be unlawful and void except when the limitation is published on an order from us.[97]

Released Rates

"Under common law, the liability of common carriers was so rigid that they were often regarded as insurers of the goods entrusted to them and it was only natural and to be expected that with the passage of time the carriers would seek ways to lessen their burdens."[98] As a result of these attempts, the courts have usually held that the carrier may limit its common law liability only by written agreement with the shipper and upon consideration of a reduced rate. The Supreme Court ruled in the Croninger case that a carrier could limit its liability by a fair, open, just, and reasonable agreement with the shipper where such agreement offered the shipper the lower of "two or more rates proportioned to the amount of risk."[99]

The reduction of liability of the carrier in the United States is limited by statute and depends upon the provision of the Carmack Amendment and the amendments represented by the first and second Cummins acts. The Carmack Amendment was judicially construed to provide for a limitation of carrier liability when the limitation was just and reasonable and evidenced by a contract fairly entered into by the shipper.[100] The second Cummins Amendment was along the same vein and section 20(11) of the Interstate Commerce Act is the statutory equivalent of these acts and cases.

The effect of the Carmack Amendment as amended by the second Cummins Amendment prohibits a carrier from limiting liability by contract with two exceptions: a "stated value" approach used in the area of baggage carried on passenger vehicles or the "released" value rate that varies with a declared or stated value.[101] Released value rates provide the shipper consideration for which in return releases the value of the goods shipped to an agreed amount. In other words, the carrier gives consideration to the shipper in the form of a reduced price[102] for shipping in return for the shipper's agreement to place a ceiling on the amount that can be recovered in the event all or part of the shipment is lost or damaged. The "declared or released value becomes the measure of the carrier's maximum liability."[103]

To obtain reduced rates in return for a limitation of liability, the shipment must be made under a written declaration of value shown on the bill of lading in accordance with rules printed in the applicable tariffs. If a writing indicating the released value of the property is not shown on the bill of lading, there must be an agreement in writing between the shipper and the carrier as to the released value of the goods in question.[104] When shipment is made under released valuation, the shipper's recovery is limited to the agreed amount unless it can be shown that "the carrier converted the property to his own use."[105]

Although the carrier cannot exempt itself from liability for its own negligence, it can limit the amount of its liability through any released rates authorized by the commission. Through this device the carrier is liable for its negligence in losing or damaging goods for the actual value thereof up to and including the agreed upon valuation as shown in the tariff. This means that the liability of the carrier for an article with an actual value of $0.30 per pound and released at a value of $0.50 per pound would be only $0.30 per pound. On the other hand, if the actual value of the article was $0.80 per pound, the maximum liability would be $0.50 per pound. Not only must released rates be expressly approved by the commission but they also must be published in tariffs and the value of goods shipped thereunder must be declared in writing by the shipper or agreed upon in writing as the released value of the property.[106]

Actual Value Rates

Actual value rates are not established for the purpose of limiting liability but are used solely to establish the value of goods for rating purposes. The actual value declared on the bill of lading does not limit liability. The carrier is still liable for the full actual value of the goods as a result of any cargo loss or damage claim. The shipper is under obligation to be certain that it specifies the actual value of goods in the bill of lading using the exact terminology shown in the carrier's tariff.[107] Actual value rates establish different rates, imposed according to the variation in the value of the articles shipped. The approval of the ICC is not required for the publication of actual value rates.

Actual value rates are not to be confused with released value rates. Under actual value rates, the carrier is liable for the full actual loss associated with the articles shipped, provided proper value has been declared by the shipper on the bill of lading in accordance with the applicable tariff provisions. The rate is established within the limits of value of the article as shown in the tariff and provides the shipper with the right to recover its full loss. There is no consideration in the form of reduced rates for a declaration by the shipper extending a maximum liability to the carrier in the form of a limitation on the amount the shipper may recover in the event of loss or damage to the shipment.

On the other hand, released rates are based on a value agreed upon between the carrier and the shipper as that amount in excess of which the carrier will not be liable in the event of loss or damage to all or any articles in the shipment. In consideration of this reduced liability, the carrier extends to the shipper a lower rate on the shipment. Under released rates the shipper assumes part of the risk of loss or damage on the movement of freight, and may obtain private insurance to cover its risk element. It is possible that the sum of the released value rate and the premium for the insurance coverage of the risk will amount to less transportation cost than the applicable unreleased rate, thus representing a savings to the shipper.

If the shipper misuses the tariff provisions applicable to actual value rates for a particular commodity by knowingly showing a value less than the actual value in order to obtain a reduced rate, its recovery in case of loss or damage may be limited to the value declared. For more practical matters, the carrier has no defense in this structure, and the shipper may claim error and submit invoices to prove higher values.

Extraordinary Value

Section 5 of the Uniform Bill of Lading, rule 15, section 2 of the National Motor Freight Classification, and rule 3 of the Uniform Freight Classification provide the authority for carriers to refuse to accept shipments of extraordinary value under certain circumstances. The problem, according to one writer, is that the carrier either does not invoke the rules because of competitive pressures from shippers of many goods in large amounts or invokes them unwisely, possibly for competitive reasons.[108] The authority is to refuse acceptance of goods because if a shipment is accepted full liability applies regardless of value. The carrier's ability to refuse shipments of extraordinary value is limited, there being only a few specific items listed in the tariffs. Apparently, no precedents exist for establishing extraordinary value.

Shipper's Responsibility

The obligation to serve the shipping public is not without limitation and the common carrier "may refuse to service poorly packed or loaded shipments since it is liable for loss or damage of freight during shipment."[109] "One of the exceptions to the carrier's common law liability arises in cases where the damage is caused by improper packing by the shipper."[110] Carriers may also refuse goods that through their inherent characteristics might contaminate other goods.[111]

Acts of negligence of the shipper under bill of lading liability for freight would include improper loading, improper packing, and concealment of the nature of goods. Failure of the shipper to comply properly with care and statutory law applicable to loading, packing, or disclosure of the nature of the product shipped may result in the loss of the right of recovery for any loss or damage to goods while in the carrier's possession.[112] "In establishing a case, the shipper must sustain the burden of proof showing that the goods were delivered to the carrier in good condition."[113]

These limitations of liability may be difficult for the carrier to establish in a court of law. "Carriers are deemed to exercise care in accepting goods for shipment and it is assumed that improperly packed or described goods would not be accepted for shipment."[114] After the carrier has accepted a shipment and issued a bill of lading without exception, the courts may hold that such acceptance constitutes an implied acknowledgment that the goods were properly packed, loaded, or described. The burden of proof would then be on the carrier to prove the loss was due to faulty packing and not carrier negligence.[115] A similar situation exists with shipper load and count shipments. If the carrier has the opportunity to observe the loading, it may be presumed it should have knowledge of any irregularities in loading procedure or improper packing. In this regard, the carrier may thus be estopped from asserting a defense of shipper fault.

In the event of a misdescription of goods on the bill of lading the shipper is liable for assessment of additional freight charges applicable to the goods shipped, if due. There is no effect on the carrier's liability.[116] However, should the shipper fraudulently misrepresent the nature of goods shipped through knowing nondisclosure of some inherent characteristic of the goods, such as perishability or a propensity to damage other goods or susceptibility to damage, the carrier may be relieved of its normal liability. The misrepresentation must be a cause of the carrier's failure to provide adequate protection.[117] "No limitations on the liability of the carrier are appropriate defenses if the carrier is guilty of contributory negligence or does not exercise due diligence."[118]

The consignee is of course responsible for accepting shipments tendered for delivery. Freight should be accepted even in a damaged condition and the carrier held responsible to whatever degree of responsibility exists. Consignees have an obligation to mitigate damages, and a breach of this obligation may be evidenced by the refusal of a shipment that is only partly damaged.[119] Another limitation of carrier liability occurs when the carrier attempts to deliver goods and is rejected by the consignee.[120] After a certain period of time and after the carrier has made reasonable efforts to deliver the goods, its liability becomes that of a warehouseman rather than that of a common carrier. "The rule is that the carrier liability becomes that of a warehouseman when the consignee refuses to accept delivery at the place specified on the bill of lading, the carrier is unable to make delivery there, or where the consignee postpones acceptance or causes delay in delivery."[121] As a warehouseman, the carrier is only required to provide care a reasonable man would give his own property.

The carrier then may be relieved of its liability as a common carrier through acts of the shipper. Specifically, such acts would include faulty packing, improper loading on shipper load and count shipments, fraudulently omitting disclosure of goods with inherently poor shipping characteristics, fraudulent misrepresentation of value (when required), and failure to accept delivery of goods. The acts of the shipper enumerated above other than unacceptance of goods must not be readily apparent. Only those acts of the shipper that would not be reasonably discovered by the carrier could be sufficient as evidence to release the carrier from its strict liability.[122]

Attempts to Limit Carrier Liability

Because of the advances in technology and the accompanying transformation of material and labor into new and innovative products, value relationships may not be comparable with the relationships existing 55 years ago. The growth of population requires a substantial corresponding growth in the flow of commodities through the transportation network. The U.S. transportation system is the most efficient in the world and has met the challenge of distributing manufactured goods to every community. Although the transportation system has evolved with changing technology and population growth, there is some evidence that there is dissatisfaction with what some may label regulatory inertia. The attempts at limiting common carrier liability as it applies to the railroads and motor carriers are evidence that some dissatisfaction exists as to the current application of common law liability to these modes of transportation.

Given the present legal and regulatory framework, there are two basic methods of providing relief to the motor carrier or railroads for the cost of cargo loss and damage expense. One method is to increase the prices of transportation on those items with high susceptibility to loss and damage in proportion to that susceptibility. When goods move at class rates, this price increase would be effected through increased classification ratings. Classification of commodities involves the grouping into a small number of classes the large number of commodities moving through trade channels today. Without classification in the present system, the pricing of transportation services would be chaotic. This process depends quite necessarily upon the use of averages; however, where a wide range of value exists within a certain class of commodity, undue price discrimination may exist. If the rating is applied at a level to provide for loss and damage expense applicable to high value goods, the low value goods must bear part of the cost. The obvious solution to this dilemma is to increase the number of rating classes. But the problem is that at the higher class levels, freight might not move and the allocation of resources is restricted.

The second approach available to the regulators for granting relief to the motor carrier and railroads common law liability is through released value ratings. This method is presently approved by regulatory agencies for use by the airlines, movers of household goods, the United Parcel Service, and the U.S. Postal Service. Released value rates are based on an agreement between the carrier and the shipper that in case of loss or damage the recovery will be limited to a stated amount, such as $0.50 per pound. The carrier, in consideration of the reduced liability, extends to the shipper the privilege of a reduced rate. The shipper may obtain the protection of carrier liability for the full value of the shipment by paying an additional rate based on the amount of excess value over a stated amount. Proponents of this method believe it is a good solution to the problem, and several plans have been submitted to the Interstate Commerce Commission for approval.

The cargo loss and damage problem is a problem for both shippers and carriers. The human element is involved, as well as the physical element. While management techniques and technology can aid in reducing cargo loss and damage, there is a point somewhere below which damage or loss cannot be prevented. In other words, a carrier's claims ratio, when viewed on a national scale, does have a minimum that is not zero and is probably a substantial amount above that figure.

Jack Stout's statement in connection with "resonances" probably reflects the thinking of many motor carriers regarding cargo damage. He contends that a carrier should not avoid its legal liability for the proper care and protection of goods during transportation, but on the other hand should not be held liable for goods lost or damaged through reasons uncontrollable by it. If the carrier has exercised due care and damage occurred for reasons beyond the reach of carrier responsibility, it should not be held liable.[123] "Resonance" would be one of the physical factors establishing the cargo loss and damage ratio at its minimum level.

Most attempts at limiting carrier liability have been in the area of released rates and with only limited success. The ICC has established criteria for the justification of need for released value ratings for a particular commodity. These criteria will be explored in more detail later in this book. The criteria most frequently named, however, are that there must be a showing that the susceptibility of the traffic to loss and damage is high and, concurrently, that the wide range of value of the commodity makes the amount of any claim difficult to estimate. There must also be available to the shipper the means of obtaining full protection at its option.[124] Some of the cases considered by the commission follow.

Ex Parte No. MC-49

The applicants in Ex Parte No. MC-49 Released Rate Rules, National Freight Classification, consisted of both rail and motor carriers. Authority was sought under section 20(11) to establish rules restricting the application of the existing class rates and ratings with certain exceptions and the initiation of rules establishing rates based on declaration of value in writing by the shipper. The motor carriers specified that rates for commodities should be based on values not to exceed \$3 per pound or \$150 per package with a maximum of \$100,000 per shipment. Rail carriers proposed an amount of \$3 per pound subject to a maximum of \$200,000 per shipment.[125]

If the shipper should desire the carrier to be fully liable for any shipment whose value was in excess of the stated limits, it could, under the proposal, obtain such coverage for an additional rate computed on the basis of \$0.10 per \$100 of excess valuation.[126] The objective was to give relief to common carriers against claims for loss and damage for items of exceptionally high value and to require shippers to disclose the value of property tendered for shipment. Such notice of value would serve to alert carriers that extra precautionary security measures might be necessary for shipments of extraordinary value. The carriers argued that inflation in prices of labor and materials, new methods of packaging, and the technology of new products such as electronic equipment had caused substantial increases in the value of commodities when compared with values in the past. An example of the problem faced by the carriers related to one 10-pound shipment of "iron and steel bolts" that was lost during shipment and was "discovered" to have a value of $60.59 per pound.

Publication of a general rule was believed to be the best available answer to the problem of liability for high valued merchandise while at the same time maintaining reasonable rates on low valued property.[127] Shippers objected to the proposal and assumed the position that the classification of commodities should reflect the increases in value and should be changed where necessary or that specific rates or ratings based on released or declared value should be established. Other objections included the difficulty shippers would experience in determining value of merchandise in mixed cases. Opponents to the proposal also contended such shipments have a wide range of value and the value may not be readily obtainable for declaration at time of shipment.[128]

As previously stated, the commission denied the application. The conclusion was accompanied by a comment that the finding did not preclude the maintenance of rates on the basis of declared or released values upon a showing of need in appropriate proceedings. This note of encouragement provides verbal solace. A study of the subsequent released rate proposals, however, shows that the commission has used its power to establish rates based on released value "sparingly."[129]

Released Value Minimum Charges

Rocky Mountain Motor Tariff Bureau, Inc., sought authority on behalf of its members to establish and maintain by tariff rule note a reduction of $0.25 per shipment on less than truckload minimum charge shipments of articles presently, or in the future, moving in straight or mixed shipments, when any or all of the articles are subject to released rates orders issued by the commission.[130] The administration law judge found the proposal just and reasonable with certain conditions, but the released rates board denied the application on appeal.[131]

In this case the carriers contended that "existing released rate and released rating orders fail to authorize carrier immunity from full liability on shipments moving at minimum charge." The limitation of carrier liability through declaration of released value by the shipper must be contingent upon consideration in the form of a price reduction offered to the shipper. A minimum charge is the lowest assessable charge for transportation, and consequently there is no alternative released value and full value charge. In order to make it clear that a reduced charge is offered on minimum shipments of commodities covered by released rate orders, the $0.25 reduction was requested.

Protestants included among their complaints to the application an assertion that savings between released value rates and full value rates on drugs amounted to roughly 18 percent and that discounts up to 75 percent were available on other articles. They asserted that Rocky Mountain's proposal offered only 1.5 to 2.6 percent discount. They further complained that the proposal was "another expensive barrier between them and the use of motor carrier LTL service,"[132] a not-too-veiled threat to resort to private carriage.

Further protestations included the omission of evidence pertaining to claims exposure on LTL traffic. In addition, they contended that the degree of discount offered in return for limited liability should be related to the cost savings experienced by carriers when their liability is restricted. "Some insight into the claims expense for the commodities affected by the released rate authority sought and the ratio of this expense to the full value freight charged purportedly is required."[133]

In its discussion and conclusions in the Rocky Mountain released value minimum charge case, there is a good exposition of the commission's expressed requirements for the approval of released rate orders.[134] Here it is noted that the authority granted the commission has been used sparingly quoting Released Rate Rules—National Motor Freight Classification, 316 ICC 499 (1962).

Quoting, Released Ratings and Rates on Engines, 47 MCC 767 (1948), where other considerations are given, including the need for a sound basis for making a definite conclusion respecting the claims rates of the commodity in question, the commission said:

> The released value should be at a normal rate or rating and should bear a reasonable relationship to the average value of the involved articles and quoting the Clothing Case, "the differential between the released and unreleased rates or ratings must bear some reasonable relationship between full and limited liability."
>
> The shipper must be provided consideration for the loss of its common law right to full recovery from the carrier in case of loss or damage . . . further, in

> addition to the normal criteria, a careful reading of the prior cases reveals other important factors that may be taken into account by the Commission. These include: the availability of insurance to the carrier; demonstrated compelling competitive circumstances; the adequacy of carrier security; a rationale for the values assigned; the existence of a "normal" unreleased rating or reasonable released rating with significant recovery.[135]

All Commodity Released Rate Proposal

In March 1975, the Middle Atlantic Conference (MAC), which represents over 1,000 carriers, petitioned the Interstate Commerce Commission for authority under sections 20(11) and 219 of the Interstate Commerce Act to establish and maintain a released valuation rule dependent on the value of certain shipments.[136] All small shipments would be covered by the rule. Applicable commodity classifications and released valuation tariff provisions would have been preempted and replaced by the proposed rule.

The Middle Atlantic Conference's expressed intentions in this specific petition included the basic assertion that pricing of shipments in the less than 1,000-pound category would be greatly simplified through the elimination of the need for rate base numbers and classification commodity descriptions. These two freight tariffs combined amount to over 900 pages of printed matter and the conference stated that "Freight charges for all distances would be reduced to two tariff pages."[137] The conference likewise contended that it was not seeking something innovative but "merely the same relief the Commission has seen fit to grant other competitive carriers."

Only two classes or rate levels were included in the proposals—"One for general commodities and the other for extremely light and bulky commodities. Within each class would be wide variations of value." The proposal was also asserted to apply to less than truckload traffic (less than 1,000 pounds), applied to property requiring expedited service, and anything that could be loaded into a van-type vehicle and delivered to all points along a truck route; and provided shippers with a simplified system of rates, tariffs, and billing. In addition, according to MAC, the proposal would result in a claims experience that would be unpredictable and any amount of loss and damage claim would be difficult to forecast. "The base amount, the amount of carrier liability, is $100 per shipment or $1.00 per pound, whichever is greater unless the shipper elects to declare a greater valuation." Greater valuations than $1 per pound would carry additional rates in the amount of $0.25 for each $1 of valuation in excess of the $100 base amount.[138] This application was denied.

On May 12, 1976, the Released Rates Board of the Interstate Commerce Commission denied authority to publish released value provisions on all shipments weighing less than 300 pounds. According to the commission, the petitioners failed to provide sufficient proof that the shipments had a wide range of value, making claims difficult to estimate; are highly susceptible to loss and damage; have a high ratio of claims to freight charges; and have a high ratio of claims to number of shipments; nor was it shown that it is difficult for carriers to obtain insurance coverage; insurance costs are unreasonably high; the relief sought is required by competition; the proposed released values are based on the fair average value of the more common forms of the involved commodities; and the proposed limited liability provisions ($50 per 100 pounds) are comparable to relief granted United Parcel Service in Released Rated Order MC-676 ($100 per 50 pounds).[139]

The ICC has applied its power to establish rates and ratings on released values sparingly. A large number of released rate proposals have recently been filed with the commission and none has been approved. This approach has been ineffective as a means of limiting carrier liability.

NOTES

1. Howard Frear, "Rate Regulation Today," ICC Practitioners Journal, June 1966, p. 777.
2. Ibid.
3. Ibid.
4. John A. Creedy, "The Built-in Bias Against Efficiency Improvement in Transportation: What to Do About It," ICC Practitioners Journal 42, no. 2 (January-February 1975): 176.
5. Gilbert J. Parr, "The Import of the Interstate Commerce Commission Studies on Railroad Freight Rates in the United States," ICC Practitioners Journal 42, no. 6 (September-October 1975): 706.
6. Roy J. Sampson and Martin T. Farris, Domestic Transportation Practice Theory and Policy, 2nd ed. (Boston: Houghton Mifflin, 1971), p. 440.
7. Creedy, op. cit., p. 177.
8. David H. Armstrong, "Focusing on Regulatory Issues," Public Utilities Fortnightly, August 27, 1970, p. 18.
9. A. H. McKinley, "Pinpointing Loss and Damage," Distribution Worldwide, March 1972, pp. 56-60.
10. Ibid.
11. Interstate Commerce Commission, Quarterly Freight Loss and Damage Claims for Quarter Ended September 30, 1975 (Washington, D.C., 1975), p. 38.

12. Interstate Commerce Commission, Released Rates Application No. MC-1228, Classification Ratings on Clothing, NOI, 349 ICC 211 (1975).

13. Ibid.

14. Sampson and Farris, op. cit., p. 440.

15. Jim Noble, "In Motion Damage Costs Carriers Dearly, Claim Council Is Told," Transport Topics, July 5, 1976, p. 1.

16. Ibid., p. 1, quoting National Freight Claim Council's Freight Loss and Damage Prevention Committee Chairman William Solak.

17. Ibid., p. 23, quoting Jack N. Stout, Jr., of National Freight Claim Council's Freight Loss and Damage Prevention Committee.

18. Miklos B. Korodi, "Terminal Security—It's a System's Job," Traffic World, April 7, 1975, p. 47.

19. McKinley, op. cit., p. 47.

20. ICC, Quarterly Freight Loss, op. cit., introductory statement.

21. "Trends in Claims Against Truckers," Distribution Worldwide, September 1971, p. 64.

22. Donald J. Bowersox, Edward W. Smykay, and Bernard J. LaLonde, Physical Distribution Management, 6th printing (New York: Macmillan, 1972), p. 160.

23. Sampson and Ferris, op. cit., p. 440.

24. Ibid.

25. Donald J. Bowersox, Logistical Management (New York: Macmillan, 1974), p. 176.

26. Charles A. Taff, Management of Physical Distribution and Transportation (Homewood, Ill.: Irwin, 1972), p. 87.

27. Ibid., p. 455.

28. Carlo J. Salzano, "Why Not a Pocketbook Approach to Cargo Loss and Damage," Traffic World, April 7, 1975, p. 27.

29. National Motor Freight Claim Council, The Claims Councillor, December 1975, p. 6.

30. 349 ICC 211.

31. Interstate Commerce Commission, Ex Parte MC-49, Released Rate Rules, National Motor Freight Classification, 316 ICC 499 (1962).

32. Interstate Commerce Commission, Released Rates Order No. MC-917, Denying Released Rates Application No. MC-1399, Intermountain Tariff Bureau, Inc. (May 1976).

33. Title 49 USC, Section 20(11).

34. Thomas R. Skulina, "Liability of a Carrier for Loss and Damage to Interstate Shipments," Cleveland-Marquette Law Review, May 1968, p. 251.

35. Richard R. Sigmon, *Miller's Law of Freight Loss and Damage Claims*, 4th ed. (Dubuque, Iowa: Brown, 1974), p. 1.
36. Sampson and Farris, op. cit., p. 103.
37. Sigmon, op. cit., p. 14.
38. Ibid., p. 79.
39. 13 C.F.R. Carriers, par. 75, p. 172.
40. Ibid., par. 90, p. 172.
41. Sigmon, op. cit., p. 270.
42. Kenneth U. Flood, *Traffic Management* (Dubuque, Iowa: Brown, 1975), p. 437.
43. Skulina, op. cit., p. 147.
44. Sigmon, op. cit., p. 270.
45. Skulina, op. cit., p. 147.
46. 13 C.J.S. Carriers, par. 71, 76-79.
47. Coggs v. Bernard (2Ld Raymond 919).
48. Ibid.
49. Sigmon, op. cit., p. 2.
50. Flood, op. cit., p. 480.
51. Sigmon, op. cit., p. 61, referencing Forward v. Pittard, 1 T.R. 27.
52. Ibid.
53. Flood, op. cit., p. 437.
54. Sigmon, op. cit., p. 3.
55. Taff, op. cit., p. 460.
56. 13 C.J.S. Carriers, par. 71.
57. Sigmon, op. cit., p. 4.
58. Taff, op. cit., p. 460.
59. 13 C.J.S. Carriers, par. 71, p. 136.
60. Skulina, op. cit., p. 251.
61. Sigmon, op. cit., p. 9.
62. Skulina, op. cit., p. 253.
63. Sigmon, op. cit., p. 10.
64. Ibid., p. 351, referencing Atlantic Coast Line v. Riverside Mills, 219 US 186; Adams Express Company v. Croninger, 266 US 491.
65. Newton Morton, "Common Law, Common Carriers and Their Transportation of Goods of Extraordinary Value," *Paper* (Kent, Ohio: Kent State University, 1967).
66. Ibid., p. 13.
67. Sigmon, op. cit., p. 15.
68. Skulina, op. cit., p. 147.
69. American Jurisprudence 2d, Carriers, par. 539, p. 67.
70. Morton, op. cit., p. 13.
71. Adams Express Company v. Croninger, 226 US 491.
72. Morton, op. cit., p. 13.

73. Ibid., p. 14, referencing William M. Mortimer, Adjusting Practices, Inland Marine and Transportation Insurance (New York: Transportation Service Company, 1951), p. 159.

74. Sigmon, op. cit., p. 10.

75. Am Jur 2d, Carriers, par. 539, p. 67.

76. Morton, op. cit., p. 14.

77. Sigmon, op. cit., p. 10.

78. Morton, op. cit., p. 14.

79. Ibid., p. 13.

80. 49 USC Section 20(11).

81. Sigmon, op. cit., p. 10.

82. Flood, op. cit., p. 482.

83. Taff, op. cit., p. 441.

84. Ibid.

85. Ibid.

86. Flood, op. cit., p. 441.

87. Sigmon, op. cit., p. 95.

88. Flood, op. cit., p. 434.

89. Ibid., p. 444.

90. Ibid., p. 446.

91. Sigmon, op. cit., p. 232.

92. Flood, op. cit., p. 479, referencing Chicago & N.W. Railroad Company v. C. C. Whitnock Produce Company, 258 US 369 (1922).

93. Ibid., p. 479.

94. 13 C.J.S. Carriers, par. 97, p. 186.

95. Sigmon, op. cit., p. 14.

96. For a listing of items in the National Motor Freight Classification 100B subject to either released rates or actual value rates, see Claims Councillor, no. 133, December 1975.

97. Sigmon, op. cit., p. 309, referencing Crown Overall Manufacturing Company v. Director General, 100 ICC 471.

98. Ibid.

99. Ibid., referencing Adams v. Croninger.

100. C.J.S. Carriers, par. 97, p. 188; Adams Express Company v. Croninger, Ky., 33 S.Ct. 148.

101. Skulina, op. cit., p. 266.

102. 13 C.J.S. Carriers, par. 95, p. 184. A lower freight rate is generally held to be sufficient consideration for a limited liability contract.

103. Sigmon, op. cit., p. 345.

104. Flood, op. cit., p. 453.

105. Ibid., p. 455, referencing Glickfield v. Howard Van Lines, 213 F 2d 723.

106. Sigmon, op. cit., p. 352.

107. Ibid., p. 309.
108. Morton, op. cit., p. 21.
109. Sampson and Farris, op. cit., p. 107.
110. Joseph C. Colquitt, _The Act and Development of Freight Classification_ (Washington, D.C.: National Motor Freight Traffic Association, 1956), p. 135.
111. Sampson and Farris, op. cit., p. 107.
112. Flood, op. cit., p. 437.
113. Skulina, op. cit., p. 254.
114. Flood, op. cit., p. 437.
115. Ibid., p. 438.
116. Skulina, op. cit., p. 255.
117. Flood, op. cit., p. 444.
118. Sampson and Farris, op. cit., p. 109.
119. Noble, op. cit., p. 23, quoting William Koch, vice president, Overnight Transportation Company.
120. Flood, op. cit., p. 482.
121. Ibid., p. 443.
122. Ibid., p. 444.
123. Noble, op. cit., p. 23, quoting Jack N. Stout, Jr.
124. Flood, op. cit., 1974, p. 453.
125. _Ex Parte No. MC-49, Released Rate Rules—National Motor Freight Classification_, 316 ICC 500.
126. Ibid.
127. Ibid.
128. Ibid.
129. Ibid.
130. _Released Rates Application No. MC-1282, Rocky Mountain Motor Tariff Bureau, Inc., Released Value Minimum Charges_, 351 ICC 505 (May 12, 1972).
131. Ibid., 351 ICC 510.
132. Ibid., 351 ICC 511.
133. Ibid., 351 ICC 512.
134. Ibid.
135. Ibid., 351 ICC 521.
136. _Released Rates Application of Middle Atlantic Conference Seeking Released Valuation Rule for Application on All Commodity Rates and Charges on Shipments Weighing Less Than 1,000 Pounds, Middle Atlantic and New England Territories_, March 3, 1975.
137. Ibid.
138. Ibid.
139. Interstate Commerce Commission, _Released Rates Order No. MC-920 (May 12, 1976), Denying Released Rates Application No. MC-1408, All Shipments Weighing Less Than 300 Pounds_.

3

RELATIONSHIP OF CARGO LOSS AND DAMAGE EXPENSE TO COSTING TRANSPORTATION SERVICE

According to contemporary law, each common carrier subject to the provisions of Title 40 of the U.S. Code is responsible for publishing rates for the movement of goods in interstate commerce. Such price lists, called tariffs, must be filed with the Interstate Commerce Commission.[1] These comprehensive statutes provide that each carrier is compelled with a duty to enforce just and reasonable rates, charges, and classifications, without undue preferences or prejudices, subject to the power of the Interstate Commerce Commission to fix reasonable rates and regulations when there are objections to the carrier's publications. The burden of proof resides with the carrier to demonstrate that any proposed rate, classification, rule, regulation, or practice is just and reasonable. Pertinent provisions of the act are as follows:

> (b) Rate, facilities for carriers of property.
>
> It shall be the duty of every common carrier of property by motor vehicle to provide safe and adequate service, equipment and facilities for the transportation of property in interstate or foreign commerce; to establish, observe, and enforce just and reasonable <u>rates</u>, charges and <u>classifications</u>, and just and reasonable practices relating thereto and to the manner of presenting, <u>marking</u>, <u>packing</u>, and delivering property for transportation, the facilities of transportation and all other matters relating to or connected with the transportation of property in interstate or foreign commerce.[2] [emphasis added]
>
> (d) Undue preferences or prejudices prohibited.
>
> All charges made for any service rendered or to be rendered by any common carrier by motor

vehicle . . . shall be just and reasonable, and every unjust and unreasonable charge for such service or any part thereof, is prohibited and declared to be unlawful. . . . It shall be unlawful for any common carrier by motor vehicle . . . to make, give, or cause any undue or unreasonable preference or advantage to any particular person, port, gateway, locality, region, district, territory, or description of traffic, in any respect whatsoever, or to subject any particular person . . . or description of traffic to any unjust discrimination or any undue or unreasonable prejudice or disadvantage in any respect whatsoever.[3] [emphasis added]

(e) Complaints to and Investigation by Commission: power of Commission to fix reasonable rates, regulations, etc.

Whenever after hearing, upon complaint or upon investigation on its own initiative, the Commission shall be of the opinion that any individual or joint rate, fare or charge . . . or any classification, rule, regulation, or practice whatsoever of such carrier or carriers affecting such rate, fare or charge . . . is or will be unjust or unreasonable, or unjustly discriminatory or unduly preferential or unduly prejudicial, it shall determine and prescribe the lawful rate, fare, or charge . . . or the lawful classification, rule or regulation . . . to be made effective.[4]

(g) At any hearing involving a change in rate, . . . or classification or in a rule or regulation or practice, the burden of proof shall be on the carrier to show that the proposed changed rate, . . . classification, rule, regulation, or practice is just and reasonable.[5]

(i) In the exercise of its power to prescribe just and reasonable rates . . . and classifications, regulations and practices, . . . the Commission shall give due consideration . . . to the inherent advantages of transportation by such carriers; to the effect of rates on the movement of traffic by the carrier or carriers for which the rates are prescribed; to the need, in the public interest, of adequate and efficient transportation service by

> such carriers at the lowest cost consistent with furnishing such service; and to the need of revenues sufficient to enable such carriers under lowest, economical and efficient management to provide such service.[6] [emphasis added]

"Under Section 5a of the Interstate Commerce Act (the so-called Reed-Bulwinkle Act, 1948) carriers were given permission to act jointly on rates and related matters, with immunity from prosecution under the antitrust statutes if agreements under which they act have the approval of the ICC."[7] Motor carriers act jointly in publishing both classification and rate tariffs through rate bureaus.

Freight bureaus are groups of carriers organized for the purpose of publishing rate tariffs, the price lists of the participating carriers. There are a number of bureaus located in various geographical locations throughout the country. Those carriers operating in the territory covered by a specific bureau usually participate in the tariffs published by the bureau. Most nonmember truckers will also participate in the tariffs. Carriers are not bound by the tariffs published by the bureaus and may establish rates through independent action.

All freight rates must be compensatory in order to be legal within the framework of administrative law. There are several factors involved in setting rates, including cost, competition, and value of service (demand). A compensatory rate must at least cover out-of-pocket (variable) cost of the carrier and make some contribution to the recovery of constant (fixed) cost of operation. There are class rates, commodity rates, and exception rates. Only class rates are discussed here, as most smaller less than truckload shipments are made under class rates.

The class rate for an average group of commodities in any particular study may be taken as the fully distributed cost plus profit.[8] Fully distributed cost is the total of variable and fixed costs. In order to establish a class rate for a particular commodity, it is necessary first to determine the rating of the commodity that denotes its shipping characteristics.[9] After determining the rating, the rate basis is determined and the appropriate rate per 100 pounds found is the rate tariff. Thus, two tariffs are necessary in order to determine a class rate, a classification tariff and a rate tariff. "The basic motor carrier independent classification system is the National Motor Freight Classification System which contains 23 classes."[10]

"Tariffs are uniform in that the contents must be arranged in the same manner. Included in the index are such items as (1) a complete list of articles on which tariff will apply if it is a commodity or exceptions tariff; (2) list of exceptions, if any, to the classification or exception tariffs to which the tariff is subject. The tariff may contain its own exceptions to the governing classification; (3) the applicable rates for the articles covered in the tariff."[11]

An important element in establishing a freight rate for the movement of a commodity in interstate commerce is its susceptibility to loss and damage. Those items that are likely to be damaged or stolen during the shipping process would receive a higher rating than those that are not so susceptible to loss or damage. "The purpose of the classification is to take into consideration characteristics of a product or a commodity that will influence cost of handling and transport."[12]

"The problem which the carrier confronts is in those instances where the highly valued goods are described in the classification or tariff,"[13] and therefore must be accepted for shipment at class rates. There may be a wide range of value within the classification description. Richard Sigmon gives an example of a carrier who accepts a shipment of machinery parts and has no knowledge of their value until they are lost or damaged. That is to say, when a claim is filed, the carrier discovers that what it perceived to be of negligible value actually has an exceptionally high value. Under present laws and regulations, the carrier is held liable for the full actual value of the goods if it has published a rating based on the description of the machine parts. The carrier is therefore deemed to have considered such value in the classification process.[14]

FREIGHT CLASSIFICATION

"Freight classification is the process of dividing articles of freight into a limited number of groups or classes for the purpose of simplifying the task of making class rates. The classification tariff also contains rules governing transport rate application."[15] Joseph Colquitt defines freight classification as a relationship. "It is an economical and practical method of equitably distributing freight charges and applying them to all articles of commerce offered for transportation by motor highway, rail, express or air service."[16]

"The primary purpose of freight classification is to assign each article, or a group of articles, to a class according to well known classification principles which recognize distinction between the articles from a transportation standpoint, along fairly broad lines. None of the principles or elements should be controlling, but all that are relevant should be considered."[17]

The classification process is a grouping process and as such must necessarily deal in averages. Within some freight classifications, one may find a wide range of value[18] among the commodities included therein. Value, of course, is an important element in classification, particularly for those commodities that are highly susceptible to cargo loss and damage. The classification of such articles in appropriately higher classes is necessary if motor carriers are to recover the cost of cargo loss and damage through the individual freight rate of such a commodity. So far there has been no formula developed that will routinely provide a classification for an item of freight, taking into consideration all the necessary characteristics that determine its relative shipping cost and transportation demand, both of which are considered in the classification process. "While classifications are mandatory, they must be just, and reasonable, and non-discriminatory and non-prejudicial."[19] "The transportation characteristics most generally considered in determining classification rating can be grouped under two broad headings: cost factors and demand factors."[20]

Flood lists elements the ICC considers in determining the proper classification of articles: bulk, character of article, competition, cost of service, desirability of traffic, distinction in transportation conditions, ease of handling, expense of carriage, hazard, liability to waste or injury, loading, manner of packing, risk, space occupied, tonnage, use, utilization of equipment, value of article, value of service, volume of traffic, and weight."[21]

"Classification is to freight rates what equity is to statutory law—flexibility as compared to rigidity."[22] The classification process is not static, and frequently commodities will undergo marked and permanent changes in their transportation characteristics such as value. When this occurs, the classification must be changed in order that equitable rates may be applied to the commodity. This was mentioned in one case as follows:

> Not infrequently commodities, and particularly manufactured commodities, undergo marked and permanent changes in their value or weight density or both and due to such developments, rates which were once on approximately the correct basis may become distinctly too high or too low.[23]

In relation to the change in a product's classification characteristics, Colquitt had this to say: "Compare today's type of machinery and agriculture instruments with those of a few years ago. Shapes, weights, sizes and values have changed; the same thing is true of furniture and store fixtures."[24]

Density

According to James Harkins, the maximum first load is approximately 46,000 pounds depending on the tare weight of the vehicle and weight laws; and, on the average, a vehicle can safely load about 2,400 cubic feet capacity.[25] Using these amounts, one may conclude that a commodity exceeding a density of between 19 and 20 pounds per cubic foot or more would deemphasize the density factor in the classification process. Thus, commodities with lower densities would exceed the 2,400 cubic foot capacity of the vehicle before reaching the optimum load weight.

In one case the National Motor Freight Traffic Association proposed on behalf of motor carriers party to the National Motor Freight Classification a new regulation providing for increased rates on LTL and actual quantity class ratings on commodities that as shipped have a density of less than 6 pounds per cubic foot.[26] The association contended that the primary transportation characteristics of a multitude of commodities have changed considerably over a period of years. Specific points mentioned included the "increased use of plastics and other lighter materials" and "the trend of packaging for display purposes in oversized containers." These two points result in decreased densities, and thus "occupy space" in motor vehicles "disproportionate to the revenue which they produce under the present ratings and rates." Because of the larger number of commodities whose shipping characteristics have changed because of these trends and the continued introduction of new articles, the association believed it impractical to revise individually its ratings and effectively separate and distinguish many varieties of the same commodity by any method other than their density differences. Under the rule the shipper would be required to measure and weigh packages in order to classify weight properly.

The ICC observed that density may deserve a heavier weighting as a factor in classifying freight because of the capacity characteristics inherent in the motor carrier industry. The agency did not, however, rule that due weight must also be given to other transportation characteristics such as value and susceptibility to loss and damage,[27] that is, "Freight of this nature (low density), if properly rated, should make its proper contribution to the transportation burden."[28]

Packing

While measuring the probability of a given article's susceptibility to loss or damage for classification purposes, packing constitutes an important factor. Packing can also have important implications pertaining to a carrier's risk and subsequent claims ratio. The reduction of loss and damage and the promotion of ease of handling both can be simultaneously accomplished through proper packaging. Indeed, good packing will give protection to the goods in transit and provide "minimum transportation risk and expense."[29]

Articles should ideally not be accepted for consignment if the commodities are not properly packed, and proper packaging includes the use of adequate outer casing with proper inner cartons or shock sustaining material. In this regard, carriers must exercise reasonable control in accepting shipments from the shipper because packages that are susceptible to damage because of poor preparation for shipment in disregard for current tariff provisions should not be accepted for transport. This exercise is a matter for carrier management and cannot be adjusted through the classification process.

"The major carrier classifications all clearly provide by rule that the carrier will refuse any article not in such condition or so prepared for shipment as to render it reasonably safe and practical for transportation." The most popular material for casing goods, according to a survey of packaging and handling engineers, was corrugated fiberboard, and this same observation is applicable to interior packing material. Seventy-five percent of respondents used outer cartons of this material and 55 percent listed the material as primary for interior packing.[30]

The classification tariffs provide by rule that articles packed in a manner rendering them unsafe for shipment will be refused by the carrier. As previously indicated, the general rule applicable is that after a carrier accepts a carton for shipment, it is generally implied that the packing is proper. Because of this, a carrier usually is not successful in demonstrating shipper's fault in the event of loss or damage to the article in question.

Volume of Traffic

Another factor entering into the classification of freight that could be termed a demand characteristic is the volume of traffic associated with a particular commodity.[31] The traffic may move in sufficient volume to lower handling cost. "For instance, large shipments frequently bypass the terminal platform and are loaded directly from the pickup and delivery vehicle into the linehaul vehicle, and the decline in cost with increases in size of shipment are quite marked."[32] Not only would cost be reduced in this instance but the direct loading into the linehaul vehicle would tend to reduce on-platform handlings, which may be advantageous from the point of view of cargo loss and damage expense. On the other hand, this particular advantage could conceivably be offset by the possibility of improper loading of the linehaul vehicle if many varied shipments are loaded randomly in the trailer.[33]

Classification Formula

"The classification of property into groups designed to fairly spread the burden of transportation has never been successfully reduced to a formula,"[34] and "no mathematical formula can be applied with any degree of authority to the determination of class percentage relationships." The problem, according to the ICC, is to arrive at relationships that will make class relationships most useful and discourage the publication of many commodity rates.[35] After noting objections to the proposed formulas in another case, the commission directed attention to the lack of consideration given to unusual high or low values, exceptional susceptibility for damage, and perhaps other factors that "will necessarily enter into the proper ratings for particular articles, for which no fixed rule can be laid down and which must be left to informed judgment."[36]

Colquitt discussed two proposals for reducing the classification process to a formula. One was suggested by the motor carrier industry in Class Rate Investigation, 1939, 262 ICC 447; yet another was devised by J. T. Ripley and was based on a unit system predicated on value and density.[37] Neither of these approaches was intended to be a complete method of classification in itself, and both were purported to be points of departure in classification from which other factors, such as susceptibility to loss and damage and method of packing, would be considered.

Colquitt provides an explanation of the difficulties involved in establishing a formula for classifying freight:

> The difficulty in arriving at any system that would be at all equitable, much less practicable, lies in the fact that in order to accomplish it, full and complete data must be had on every type of each and every one of the thousands of commodities listed in the classification, which information is by no means easy of access. Moreover, values, weights, competition, etc., are constantly changing.[38]

In this regard, perhaps released rates represent the optimum solution to this problem.

RELEASED VALUE RATINGS

Section 20(11) of the Interstate Commerce Act provides that the Interstate Commerce Commission has the authority to establish rates based on the released value of an article moving in interstate commerce. Those commodities for which released ratings exist are shown in the classification tariffs. An article moving under a classification providing for a released value is in legal effect a "distinct and separate commodity" from the same commodity moving under a classification that does not provide for a released value.[39] "Released and unreleased ratings should be considered from a transportation standpoint as separate and distinct items."[40]

In this regard, Flood provides a comprehensive definition of released rates:

> A released value rate is a rate based on a declared value in writing by the shipper or agreed upon by the shipper and the carrier. When released rates are published, the shipper is given the choice of several rates. Under the lower rates, the shipper, in consideration of the reduced rate, declares and agrees that for purposes of claim in case of loss or damage, the value of his shipment is not in excess of a certain amount.[41]

In Released Rates on Stone in the Southeast,[42] the philosophy behind released rates was cogently expressed by the commission. The agency pointed out that frequent loss and damage claims on a given commodity are not of sufficient weight to require the establishment of released rates. Given a reasonable range of value within the commodity group, the carrier should establish appropriate ratings to recover losses due to loss and damage. Neither is the fact that an article has a wide range of value alone sufficient to justify released rates, as claims loss may be negligible. "But where those conditions concur, where the susceptibility to loss and damage is comparatively high and the wide ranges of value makes the amount of any claim that might arise difficult to estimate, the carrier is at a disadvantage unless it is permitted to base its liability and its charges on a declaration of value obtained in advance from the shipper."[43] According to Newton Morton, it was in this case that the primary requirement that the "simultaneous existence of a high frequency of claims and a wide range of value within the commodity group" was established.[44] The four main criteria for evaluating proposals for released rates or ratings have evolved through the years, and while these criteria are not exclusive, the Released Rates Board expects applicants to bear the proof of them.

In Classification Ratings on Clothing,[45] the Commission quotes Wearing Apparel, Accessories, Piece Goods—Shulman, Inc.,[46] in giving a summary of the four core criteria:

> Before any partial exemption can be granted, certain criteria must be met. They are: (1) That the wide range of value in the commodity makes the amount of any claim that may arise difficult to estimate, (2) that the susceptibility of the traffic to loss or damage is relatively high, (3) that a high ratio of claims to freight charges exists, and (4) that a great number and frequency of claims for loss and damage exists.[47]

Other criteria mentioned by the commission in denying Classification Ratings on Clothing included its finding that the applicants had not shown that there was difficulty in obtaining adequate insurance or that the cost of insurance was unreasonably high, or that they should be allowed to maintain released rates in order to foster competition.[48] The procedure enumerated in section 20(11) of the Interstate Commerce Act is the only legal method by which a carrier may limit its liability for less than the full actual loss or damage or injury to freight.[49] Indeed, one purpose of maintaining released rates is to limit carrier liability in return for the consideration of lower rates to the shipper. Another purpose mentioned by the Middle Atlantic Conference in its proposal for blanket-released value rates on small shipments is in turn the simplification of a carrier's billing process with lower costs.[50]

The reduced rates achieved through the combination of shifting of liability for cargo loss and damage and savings in operating costs could be substantial if some form of released rate or ratings plans was initiated for small shipments. The managerial question, of course, is whether or not the amount of rate savings would offset the total claims paid by the respective shippers. If a firm's claims experience remained relatively constant after the new plan was instigated, the savings in indirect cost could be a real gain to the shipping public in the form of lower shipping cost. Only if the claims experience increased could such a plan be considered unprofitable. Shippers have in general protested that a blanket-released rates method of pricing transportation service would result in a reduction in carrier claims prevention and security measures. In answering such objections, the commission stated that "the intense competition prevailing in transportation ensures that a carrier can ignore the necessity for care in handling traffic only at the peril of losing needed business."[51]

COSTING TRANSPORTATION SERVICES

"The Supreme Court has directed that outlays that are exclusively applicable to a particular class of traffic must be assigned to that traffic and that the other expenses must be fairly apportioned."[52] With this decision, the Supreme Court rendered to the regulatory agencies and carriers dealing with freight rates a problem for which there is no perfect solution. The age-old difficulties in selecting volume bases for allocation of fixed cost are present, but another problem is the assignment of variable cost to various segments of traffic. The joint cost problem is inherent in transportation costing and no one has yet arrived at a completely satisfactory method for solving the problem.[53]

The importance of proper allocation of cost to various segments of transportation may be emphasized by reference to section 216(g) of the Interstate Commerce Act. This law imposes upon motor carriers the burden of proving, at any hearing, that proposed rates are just and reasonable. Whether or not a proposed rate is granted may depend on the ICC's decision as to whether or not the rate is compensatory to the carrier. In one proceeding, a carrier's rates were found not just and reasonable because of the omission of several cost factors, such as repairs and servicing, and cargo loss in the computation of variable costs connected with the traffic in question.[54] In yet another rate docket the inclusion of an allowance for loss and damage based on data prepared by an ICC cost finding section resulted in out-of-pocket costs that were 101.8 percent of the competitive rate proposed by a railroad. In this regard, the commission concluded that the proposed rate was not compensatory and not shown to be just and reasonable.[55]

The allocation of cost to segments of traffic and to the function of carrier operations is no easy task. The new Uniform System of Accounts for Class I and Class II Motor Carriers of Property adopted by the ICC that became effective January 1, 1974 should assist carriers significantly in accounting for their costs. Motor carrier cost "can be determined largely although not entirely by methods of conventional accounting or direct observation."[56] John Meyers, moreover, suggests that fixed costs are insignificant in the cost structure of the individual motor carrier and that their "technology creates relatively linear and divisible cost functions." Changes in cost, according to Meyers, may be accomplished by the addition or subtraction of single production units, such as a truck or trailer.[57] Meyers states that in large part the rate structure in the United States does not adequately reflect the cost variations caused by size and distance of shipment.

The cost behavior in the trucking industry is characterized by decreasing cost per ton or hundredweight as the size of the shipment increases. This is explained by the fact that each shipment involves a fixed billing and collecting charge and a fixed running time and contact time during pickup and delivery, and spreading this cost over an increasing number of tons results in a small cost per ton.[58] Because of this, truck profits are realized largely on the larger size and longer haul shipments. Because of this relationship and the fact that losses are experienced on the small size short-haul traffic, the short-haul small shipment problem is created.[59]

The Interstate Commerce Commission, through Ex Parte No. MC-98, has opened the door for carriers and shippers and all interested parties to submit proposals for suggestions that might improve the applicability of cost evidence to rate restructuring proposals. This is a move in the direction of finding a solution to the problem.

UNIFORM SYSTEM OF ACCOUNTS

The Interstate Commerce Commission has developed a new System of Accounts for Class I and Class II Common and Contract Motor Carriers of Property.[60] Various accounts have been developed to aid in developing information for management and regulatory agencies in the area of cargo loss and damage expense. Activities, moreover, have been defined along functional lines in conformity with motor carrier operating practices. A proper use of any accounting system should provide information about cargo loss and damage heretofore unavailable to management or regulators. But problems remain present with reference to individual carrier responsibilities in designing their own systems to provide information for assignment to the functional activities associated with cargo loss and damage expense. This assignment of expense to the various activities in most instances requires additional record maintenance by some carriers. In any event, significant improvement has been achieved in the treatment of cargo loss and damage expenses in accounting records over the previous method of including those expenses in general and administrative accounts with an allocation on a per-dollar basis.

Some question remains as to the proper handling of indirect expenses associated with the cargo loss and damage efforts. Such expenses as motor vehicle use in the inspection process, fees paid independent inspection agencies, salaries of management and clerical personnel involved in handling claims, computer time, and depreciation on building and office equipment are among inordinate costs related to cargo loss and damage. The system of accounts fails to provide specific account numbers for cargo loss and damage in general and administrative expense. The cost of cargo loss and damage is an important element in the rate-making process, and the fact that the commission must render judgments relative to whether or not proposed new rating plans could contribute to increased efficiency in the establishment of rates and in claims administration indicates that knowledge of these costs conceivably could be helpful. Under the present system these indirect costs could be accumulated in the account cargo loss and damage expense, terminal.

Activities

"'Activity' applies to the cost groupings to which operating expenses shall be distributed." The regulation provides for section A activities, which are those applicable to instruction 27 and instruction 28 carriers. Instruction 27 carriers are those "which derive an average of 75 percent or more of their operating revenues from the intercity transportation of general commodities." Instruction 28A carriers include all other carriers except those subject to instruction 27 and carriers of household goods.[61]

This study limits the exploration of activities and the associated distribution of expenses to Class I and Class II common carriers of general commodities that fall within the jurisdictional purview of instruction 27 of 49 CFR 1207. The distribution of expenses by these carriers are to be made to the following activities: linehaul, pickup and delivery, billing and collecting, platform, terminal, maintenance, traffic and sales, insurance and safety, and general and administrative. These activities are identified in the standard system of accounts by the unit position of the account numbers that correspond to the numbers shown for each activity.[62]

The accounts involved in accounting for cargo loss and damage insurance expense have been significantly expanded by the commission to a basis that is more reflective of the cause-and-effect relationships inherent in the loss and damage experience of motor carriers. Prior to 1974 this expense was charged to general overhead and allocated on a dollar basis to the activities of linehaul, pickup and delivery, terminal platform, and billing and collecting. Effective January 1, 1976, provisions have been made for the direct allocation of cargo loss and damage insurance to the activities of linehaul, pickup and delivery, and platform and terminal. This allocation is made directly through the use of accounts 4821, cargo loss and damage insurance linehaul; 4822, cargo loss and damage insurance expense pickup and delivery; 4824, cargo loss and damage insurance expense platform; and 4825, cargo loss and damage insurance terminal. These accounts are illustrated in the matrix of operating expenses for instruction 27 and 28A carriers.[63]

Clarification of the procedures to be used by motor carriers in allocation of cargo loss and damage insurance expense to activities may be determined by referring to the Supplement to Classes I and II Motor Carrier Annual Report Forms. In this particular supplement, item 2 was headed allocation of cargo loss and damage insurance expense assigned to account 4825 to pickup and delivery and platform services. Under the Uniform System of Accounts in effect for 1974, all cargo loss and damage insurance expense was charged to accounts 4821, linehaul, and 4825, terminal. Carriers, moreover, were instructed that, for cost purposes, account 4825 was to be allocated further to pickup and delivery and platform service to account for the portions of premiums paid and estimated liabilities accrued that were applicable to loss and damage of freight while in pickup and delivery vehicles or occurring at the platform.[64]

A brief explanation of the activities is provided in part 1207 applicable to instruction 27 carriers. The definitions of the activities involved in the allocation of cargo loss and damage expense are as follows:

> (1) "Linehaul": This activity refers to the physical transportation of traffic between intercity terminals or enroute . . . it excludes cost incurred while performing pickup and delivery or peddle service.
>
> (2) "Pickup and Delivery": This activity refers to the physical operation for assembly or distribution from terminals, either in picking up freight from shippers and connecting carriers or delivering freight to consignees or connecting carriers. It includes such items as:
>
> (a) All costs incurred from the time the vehicle leaves the carrier's terminal to pickup or deliver freight until it returns to the terminal.
>
> (b) Expense incurred in peddle trips.[65]
>
> (4) "Platform": This activity refers to the handling of freight at the carrier's platform.
>
> (5) "Terminal": This activity refers to the operation at the carrier's terminal. It includes such items as:
>
> (a) Salaries and wages of employees within the terminal the cost of which is not provided elsewhere.
>
> (b) Operating supplies.
>
> (8) "Insurance and Safety": This activity refers to the administration of insurance (other than employee bene-

> fit programs), approval and payment of freight claims, and directing the safety program. It includes such items as:
>
> (a) Salaries and wages of employees administering the insurance, claims and safety programs for the carrier.
>
> (b) Premiums and costs of self insurance covering liability.
>
> (c) Expenses incidental to operating an insurance department.[66]

Paragraph (3)(4) of instruction 27 stipulates that automobiles used by the safety department employees making inspection trips will be assigned to the insurance and safety activity.[67]

Cargo Loss and Damage Insurance

> Periodic charges to expense accounts for the purpose of estimating liability for self insurance shall be determined currently by the carrier from its best source of information and the rates used may be based on percentage of revenue, mileage of vehicles, amounts of payrolls, or other equitable basis.[68]

Instruction 22, insurance, of 49 CFR 1207 provides for the charging of premiums paid to insurance companies for cargo loss and damage insurance to account 4820, cargo loss and damage insurance. The charges for any related estimated liabilities for self-insurance of the cargo loss and damage risk should also be made to this account. The estimated liability for self-insurance of cargo loss and damage is credited to account 2173, cargo loss and damage claims.[69]

The expense account group controlled by account 4820, cargo loss and damage insurance, "includes the net cost (premium less dividends or refunds) of commercial insurance to protect the carrier against liability for claims resulting from loss or damage to, or delay of, property entrusted to it for transportation and storage. Also included in this account is the estimated expense associated with the establishment of the amount to be credited to account 2173 as explained above. The total of cargo loss and damage insurance expense is reflected in the control account, 4820, and will contain the total of the amounts charged to the above-mentioned expense accounts.[70]

Indirect Costs of Handling Cargo Loss and Damage

The matrix of operating expenses for instruction 27 carriers illustrates that depreciation furniture and office equipment is not allocated to insurance and safety but to linehaul, pickup and delivery, billing and collecting, platform, terminal, and maintenance and the balance to general and administrative expense.[71] Other accounts handled in the same manner include 4830, insurance on buildings or structures, 5310, depreciation buildings and structures, and 5370, improvements to lease-hold property. Other costs that are associated indirectly with cargo loss and damage would include computer time, salaries and wages, and automobile expenses. As previously stated, the isolation of these costs on some reasonable basis of allocation could be beneficial in making appraisals of the total cost of cargo loss and damage to carriers.

Freight Claims Records

Paragraph (e) of instruction 22, insurance, of the Uniform System of Accounts 49 CFR 1207 provides the information requirements to be shown by freight claim records. The records are to be maintained so as to show for each loss and damage claim received the claims number, date and amount, the waybill or expense bill number and the date, name of claimant, kind of commodity, whether the weight is less than 10,000 pounds or over 10,000 pounds, date claim was paid or date claim was disallowed and reasons, amount of salvage recovered, amount reimbursed by insurance companies, connecting carriers or others, and the amount absorbed by the carrier. "Each claim received shall be entered in the records and should be supported by the complete file of claim papers." In the event the claims records are retained by an insurance company or another carrier an "acknowledgement by the party retaining the file that the papers are in its possession" should be obtained. The section also provides that overcharge claims and cargo loss and damage claims shall not be intermingled in the carrier's records.[72]

PRINCIPLES AND PRACTICES FOR THE INVESTIGATION AND VOLUNTARY DISPOSITION OF LOSS AND DAMAGE CLAIMS AND PROCESSING SALVAGE

Regulations Covering Freight Loss and Damage Claims

Regulations contained in the Code of Federal Regulations govern the processing of loss and damage claims derived from loss, damage, injury, or delay to property transported in interstate or foreign commerce by motor common carriers as well as for other common carriers. The regulations, moreover, establish the rules pertaining to the filing of claims, acknowledgment of claims, investigation of claims, disposition of claims, and processing of salvage property.[73]

Claims must be filed in writing with either the delivering or originating carrier or with the carrier on whose line the specified "loss, damage, injury or delay occurred" within certain time limits as required by law. Minimum filing requirements include a written communication from the claimant identifying the shipment of property, asserting liability for the loss, and making claim for "a specified and determinable amount of money." This separate written communication from the claimant is required to constitute a claim, and other supporting documents to the claim, such as inspection reports and bills of lading, are not instruments sufficient to comply with the requirements.[74]

Either payment, declination, or acknowledgment of a properly filed claim must be provided to the claimant by the respective carrier in writing within 30 days of receipt. If any additional documentation or information is required by the carrier before further consideration of the claim, the acknowledgment must give notice of these requirements. Also, the carrier is compelled to maintain a separate file for each claim received and in turn must assign successive claims file numbers in addition to noting that file numbers are specified on all correspondence and documents pertaining to the claim. Unless the internal procedure for processing claims is such that unlawful duplicate payment of claims is prevented, the carrier is required to note the claims file number on the shipping order and delivery receipt, if these are in the carrier's possession.

Prompt investigation of claims is stipulated and the investigation must include the necessary supporting documents, including the original bill of lading, evidence of freight charges, and evidence to support the prices and values of the claimed items. If proper documentation of shipment value is not furnished by the claimant, the carrier must require it to certify to the destination value of the involved freight in writing. In the case of a claim for loss, the claimant must certify in writing that the property has not been received from another source.[75]

Carriers subject to the Interstate Commerce Act are required to dispose of properly filed claims for loss or damage through payment, declining to pay, or compromise settlement offer within 120 days after receipt of the claim. If the claim cannot be processed within this finite period of time, the carrier must advise the claimant concerning the status of the claim at the end of each succeeding 60-day period during which the claim remains outstanding.[76] Any undelivered property due to refusal or rejection by the consignee on account of claimed damage may be disposed of by the carrier after proper notice to interested parties by selling, disposal, or through a salvage agent. The carrier is legally required to maintain proper records of the property disposed of in this manner for indexing the data to the shipment and claim involved. Any such disputed property shall be assigned a lot number, which number is noted on "its record of shipment and claim, if any claim is filed thereon." The carrier is required to "dispose of property in a manner that will fairly and equally protect the best interest of all persons having an interest therein."[77]

Quarterly Loss and Damage Report: Schedule A, Form QL&D

Schedule A must be completed by common carriers of general freight. But other carriers required to report loss and damage statistics, such as contract carriers, do not complete schedule A but report their experience for the quarter in schedules B and C. Common carriers of general freight report all freight loss and damage claims paid during a calendar quarter by number of claims paid by dollar amount by commodity. Claims are further subdivided in schedule A of the quarterly loss and damage report by cause of claim. In this regard, the causes of loss and damage claims are in turn categorized into seven classifications: shortage; theft and pilferage; hijacking; concealed damage; visible damage; wreck and catastrophe; and delay, heat, cold, water, or other.

Interline claims are reported as a claim in the dollar amount paid to the connecting carrier. The dollar amounts paid to claimants should be adjusted to the reporting carrier's portion of the liability for loss.[78] Claims paid by a carrier's insurance company are also reported as if the claim were paid directly by the carrier.[79]

The specific commodity breakdown is predicated on the same commodity code numbers and descriptions as those employed in reporting freight commodity statistics, 49 CFR 1248. The codes are derived from the Standard Transportation Commodity Code (STCC) with an additional code for miscellaneous freight shipments not otherwise indexed,[80] and the STCC is used for reporting freight commodity statistics.[81]

Quarterly Report of Freight Loss and Damage Claims: Schedule B, Analysis of Theft, Form QL&D

The payment and reporting of claims in schedule B, due to theft, is the individual responsibility of the carrier on whose line the theft occurred and any claim paid during the quarter in excess of $100 known to be a result of theft and pilferage or hijacking is reported individually by commodity.[82] Lastly, commodity descriptions are obtained from the freight bill under which the consignment was transported and are assigned appropriate code numbers specified in schedule A instructions. The location where the theft occurred is coded in schedule B by standard codes as provided in the report and designates either the commercial zone or state or foreign country (Canada or Mexico) where the theft is reasonably suspected to have occurred.[83]

Quarterly Report of Freight Loss and Damage Claims: Motor Schedule C, Analysis of Claims Processed, Form QL&D

Schedule C, analysis of claims processed—all carriers, must be completed by all carriers filing Form QL&D, and provides an analysis of the claims processed by a carrier during a quarter. Provisions are made, moreover, for reporting the number of claims on hand at the beginning of the quarter, the number received or reopened during the quarter by number and dollar amount, and the number and amount of claims paid, denied, or closed during the quarter.[84] The amounts recovered as a result of claims during the quarter in the form of salvage or insurance and the net claims paid during the quarter after such moneys in addition to the carrier's ratio of net claims to total revenue for the quarter are likewise reported in schedule C together with the cost of cargo insurance paid to outside insurance companies for the quarter.[85]

In addition to the above information, schedule C provides for an analysis of the carrier's timeliness in payment of claims, dividing the number of claims into those paid or denied within 30 days, those paid or denied 30 to 120 days, and those unsettled more than 120 days on hand at the close of the quarter.[86]

Quarterly Report of Freight Loss and Damage Claims: Motor (Form QL&D) Certification

Certification that Form QL&D was prepared in "accordance with effective rules as promulgated by the Interstate Commerce Commission" and that the report is "a full, true and correct statement of the freight loss and damage statistics" of the carrier for the quarter is to accompany the report in the space provided.

PROCEDURES IN REVENUE PROCEEDINGS

In Ex Parte No. MC-82,[87] the Interstate Commerce Commission solicited public comments on proposed new procedures governing the data and information to be submitted by motor carriers in proceedings involving general rate increases. The stated purpose was not to limit the amount of information presented but to reduce the time required for ultimate disposition, achieve greater uniformity in data submitted, and provide adequate notice to carriers and the public of minimum evidence deemed necessary for a decision.[88]

A review of Ex Parte No. MC-82 demonstrates that additional modifications in the procedures have been made. The amended or modified procedures provide that an "entire evidential case" be filed when a proposed rate increase on specific traffic results in an increase in annual revenue of the applicant carriers in the amount of $1 million or more. This includes either general rate increases or rate restructuring cases amounting to an increase of $1 million or more. Carriers are legally required to file in addition to tariff schedules a case consisting of a traffic study, a cost study, and revenue need.[89]

The regulations are specific in the explanation of the information to be provided in an entire evidential case. The following scenario provides an overview, including a number of the requirements. For example, a rate restructuring involving an increase in revenue of less than $1 million would require a traffic study and a cost study, in addition to revenue need.[90] Also, whenever tariff schedules other than those described above are filed by rate bureaus or carriers, they must be prepared to comply with whatever procedures the ICC "may direct in the event an investigation is instituted."[91]

Traffic Study

The traffic study that must be submitted to incorporate the most current 12-month year available was selected after consideration of the effective date of the tariff schedules involved in accordance with the regulations. In any event, the traffic study data for the immediately preceding calendar year will be employed if physically available. This most current 12-month year as selected will become the "base calendar year actual" in the study, and "the study shall include a probability sampling of the actual traffic handled during identical time periods for each study carrier."[92]

The study carriers shall consist of instructing 27 carriers "who participate in one of the motor carrier industry's Continuing

Traffic Studies" deriving at least $1 million in revenue from the issue traffic or at least 1 percent of the total operating revenues of all carriers from the issue traffic.[93] In this regard:

> (c)(3) Respondents shall also submit the following statistical data relative to the components of the sample: (1) The number of single-line shipments and the revenue derived therefrom for a) the total traffic (issue and non-issue), and b) the issue traffic only; (2) The number of interline shipments and revenues derived therefrom for a) the total traffic (issue and non-issue), b) the issue traffic only; (3) The number of interline "segments" carried by the non-study carriers and revenues derived therefrom for a) the total traffic (issue and non-issue), and b) the issue traffic only.[94] [emphasis added]

The carried basis, or only that issue traffic handled solely by the study carriers, either single line or interline, is to be used for cost and revenue purposes. The through basis may be submitted also but must be substantiated statistically.[95]

Cost Study

The federal regulations provide that Highway Form B may be employed for the purpose of the required cost study. "Service unit cost must be developed for each individual study carrier, adjusted by size of shipment and length of haul and shall be applied to respective individual carriers traffic service units as developed from its traffic study." Operating ratios for the issue traffic by weight brackets affected by the rate proposal will be determined for the traffic study year, a "present pro forma year," and a "restated pro forma year." The "present pro forma year" is based on "present wage price and productivity levels prevailing on a date no later than 45 prior to the date of the tariff filing." The "restated pro forma year" is based on "provable wage, price and productivity levels prevailing on the effective date of the proposed rates." Operating ratios are to be illustrated for this "restated pro forma year" based on current revenues, as well as on proposed revenues.[96] The cost study is also used to provide certain required useful revenue-cost comparisons.[97] For the purpose of determining operating ratios and the revenue-cost comparisons required in appendix A, "the 'each to each' costing method is used for the purpose of demonstrating base calendar year actual figures."

The "each to each" costing method refers to the "application of each individual study carrier's unit cost to its traffic service units." Provisions for updating the "base calendar year actual" figures are accomplished by using individual carrier data or through the use of composite carrier updating data. Component carrier data may be obtained from grouping those individual study carriers whose issue traffic for the "base calendar year actual" amounts to at least 50 percent of their individual total system revenues or through a grouping of that group of carriers whose total issue traffic revenue for the "base calendar year actual" amounts to at least 50 percent of all study carriers' issue revenue.[98]

Revenue Need

> Traffic and cost study carriers . . . shall submit evidence of the sum of money, in addition to operating expenses, including that needed to attract debt and equity capital, which they require to insure financial stability and the capacity to render service.[99]

In addition to the traffic study, cost study, and the submission of revenue need, the applicants shall submit a summary of the proposal including a general designation of the increase proposed, its effective date, geographic scope, and amount of insurance and supporting rationale for the increase along with conclusions reached in the traffic study and cost study and effect of transactions of affiliates on the parent revenue need.[100] A news release representing notice of the increase proposal is required to be submitted to the commission suitable for printing in a newspaper.[101]

Ex Parte No. MC-98

Ex Parte No. MC-98 instituted a proceeding initiated by the ICC for the purpose of amending paragraph 1104.3 of Title 49 of the Code of Federal Regulations, which prescribes procedures for the required cost study in motor carrier revenue proceedings as described in the previous section of this chapter. Also, the proceeding is for the additional purpose of "reviewing representation or suggested procedures to be followed by motor carriers filing tariffs incorporating restructuring proposals."[102] "The present motor carrier LTL rate structure is essentially a copy of the classification based system developed, and still used, by rail carriers." Except for the coordinated classification, a volume-density-related system developed by New England carriers, all rate bureaus use basically the same system of rate making based on "classification as the basis for differentiating between the relative transportability of different commodities."[103]

The introduction of Ex Parte MC-98 stipulates that this classification of products on the basis of transport characteristics functioned adequately when motor carriers were able to apply value of service factors in determining classifications of commodities. In the early days the motor carriers were able to attract profitable LTL traffic through rates and service. The commission noted, however, that the common carrier trucking industry is in an analogous position formerly occupied by the railroads. Competition has directed the shipments of high values of service rates and left the motor carrier with the unsubsidized less profitable traffic.[104]

The problem as stated by MC-98 in the case of LTL service revolves around a "continuing need there for . . . rates which on the one hand will enable shippers to continue to utilize existing service, and on the other hand, insure that the trucking industry will be able to offer the service at a reasonable profit." The commission expresses concern over the motor carrier's ability to continue to meet the needs of the public for LTL service and asks for "public comment and suggestions with respect to (1) the need for, or (2) the desirability of, or (3) ways and means of restructuring the less-than-truckload and small shipment rate structure presently applicable on traffic moving by motor carriers."

Individual comments, according to the commission, were not to be "confined necessarily to modification of the present traditional rate structure." The commission is searching for comments from all interested parties to propose either improvements to the present rate-making process or to proffer a completely new system for pricing small shipments. The functional objective of the ICC is to provide service to the shipper at a price it can afford and at a price that will return a profit to the motor carrier industry.[105]

In Ex Parte MC-98 the commission requested comments to all or some of the "general matters" as specifically indicated below:

> (1) What problems, if any, have you experienced in connection with LTL or small shipment traffic? If you have experienced any problems, e.g., in costs, service, handling, or other, would you please describe them in detail? Can, or should anything be done to change, improve, or replace the present LTL and small shipment rate structure?

(2) Can action be taken to increase the volume of small shipment traffic, other than subsidization by other traffic?

(3) Are there any alternatives to the present physical methods of handling LTL and small shipments by carriers which could, or should, replace current methods?

(4) In light of the criticism of shippers that motor common carriers do not provide adequate small shipment service, and the complaints of carriers that the existing rate structure does not compensate them adequately for the cost of handling small shipment traffic, what can be done to reconcile the need for an adequate rate structure for motor carriers and the need for LTL rates which shippers can afford to pay?

(5) Where certain shippers, industries, or localities have no alternative means of transportation and require LTL service, is there a point at which the carrier burden should be deemed to outweigh the need for the service?

(6) Could, or should, alternative rates based on differing service needs, e.g. expedited, standard, and standby, be offered for LTL service? How could, or should, such alternative rates be constructed?

(7) If you feel certain commodities or classes or traffic are unfairly priced under the existing rate structure, please give specific examples, and suggest how this unfairness can, or should be eliminated.

The restructuring of freight rates "can take the form of a proposal to increase different weight categories of freight by various percentages or it can take the form of a proposal to reduce rates applicable on certain weight brackets while increasing rates on other weight brackets."[106] The commission, moreover, proposes that the procedures prescribed in 49 CFR 1104 do not provide for the determination of ratios for various weight brackets of freights. The omission of such data may possibly prevent the full commission from considering what might constitute an important item in rendering a decision relative to whether or not any proposed rate restructuring results in just and reasonable freight rates for carriers to assess and shippers and receivers to pay.

Under the proposed amendments, procedure would be modified to show operating ratios for the following weight brackets:

		Pounds
1.	Minimum charges less than truckload	
2.		1-199
3.		200-499
4.		500-999
5.		1,000-1,999
6.		2,000-4,999
7.		5,000-9,999
8.		10,000 and over
9.	Total LTL (Lines 2 through 8)	
10.	Total minimum charges and LTL (Lines 1 & 9)	
11.	Truck load	
12.	Total all shipments (Lines 10 & 11)[107]	

The proposed revision to 49 CFR 1104.3 provides for ratios to be updated employing appendix E, parts I and II, of Ex Parte MC-98 (see Figures 2 and 3).

Completion of the data in Figure 3 provides the dollar amounts of revenue and expense to substantiate the calculation of operating ratios that are presented in Figure 2. Information is shown in these two figures for both issue traffic and nonissue traffic. Base calendar year actual, present pro forma year, and restated pro forma operating ratios are submitted. The present pro forma year is based on present wage, price, and productivity levels prevailing no later than 45 days after filing the rate restructuring proposal. Restated pro forma year figures are based on provable wage, price, and productivity levels that will exist on the date the proposed rates are to be effective. This restatement is presented for both current and proposed revenues.

Some academicians and theoreticians blame value of service pricing for the railroad's demise, and all would agree that in the long run adequate profits were not earned by the railroads to attract investment capital or to provide for replacement of plant equipment out of earnings.[108] Conceivably, the motor common carrier of general commodities may be the next victim of any rate structure associated with value of service pricing. As competition intensifies the freight market and high profit traffic is diverted to other modes, motor carriers may experience a corresponding increase in operating ratios and the relationship between revenues and profits. Should pricing practices in the motor carrier industry convert to a cost-oriented basis, cost will become more important in pricing freight transportation service and a new primary formula will be necessary.

FIGURE 2

Part I: Operating Ratios by Standard Weight Brackets on Issue and Nonissue Traffics
(Carried traffic basis)

Line No.	Standard Weight Brackets 1/	Base Calendar Year—Actual			Present Pro forma Year	Restated Pro forma Year	
		Issue Traffic 2/	Non-Issue Traffic: Territorial Traffic Related to Issue Traffic But Not Affected by Rate Proposal 3/	Non-Issue Traffic: All Other Non-Issue Traffic 4/	Issue Traffic Only 5/	Based on Current Revenues (Issue Traffic Only 5/)	Based on Proposed Revenues (Issue Traffic Only 5/)
	(1)	(2)	(3)	(4)	(5)	(6)	(7)
1	Minimum Charges						
	Less Than Truckload (pounds)						
2	1-199						
3	200-499						
4	500-999						
5	1,000-1,999						
6	2,000-4,999						
7	5,000-9,999						
8	10,000 and over						
9	Total LTL (Lines 2 thru 8)						
10	Total Minimum Charges and LTL (Lines 1 and 9)						
11	Truckload						
12	Total, All Shipments (Lines 10 and 11)						

Source: Interstate Commerce Commission, *New Procedures in Motor Carrier Restructuring Proceedings Notice of Proposed Rule Making, Ex Parte MC-98* (1975).

FIGURE 3

Part II: Expenses and Revenues Supporting Operating Ratios in Part I
(Dollars in thousands)

		Base Calendar Year - Actual											
				Non-Issue Traffic									
								Present Pro forma Year		Restated Pro forma Year			
										Based on Current Revenues		Based on Proposed Revenues	
										Issue Traffic Only			
Line No.	Standard Weight Brackets	Issue Traffic		Territorial Traffic Related to Issue Traffic But Not Affected By Rate Proposal		All Other Non-Issue Traffic							
		Expenses	Revenues	Expenses	Revenues	Expenses	Revenues	Expenses	Revenues	Expenses	Revenues	Expenses	Revenues
	(1)	(2)	(3)	(4)	(5)	(6)	(7)	(8)	(9)	(10)	(11)	(12)	(13)
1	Minimum Charges												
	Less Than Truckload (pounds)												
2	1-199..................												
3	200-499................												
4	500-999................												
5	1,000-1,999............												
6	2,000-4,999............												
7	5,000-9,999............												
8	10,000 and over												
9	Total LTL (Lines 2 thru 8).................												
10	Total Minimum Charges and LTL (Lines 1 and 9)												
11	Truckload.............												
12	Total, All Shipments (Lines 10 and 11)												

Source: Interstate Commerce Commission, *New Procedures in Motor Carrier Restructuring Proceedings Notice of Proposed Rule Making, Ex Parte MC-98* (1975).

The prevailing attitude of the judiciary and the regulatory agencies toward carrier liability relative to the motor carrier industry has been static to a significant degree. Other modes of transportation have simplified rate structures that in part may be attributable to the shifting of cargo loss and damage liability through the avenue of released value rates or ratings. A new, bold, and innovative approach to freight liability in the motor carrier industry could result in lower freight costs to the shipping public and contribute to diminishing inflation.

In reference to this static adherence to tradition, Sigmon writes: "This tending to adhere to rules long after the reason for the rules have disappeared results in a rigidity in the law, a rigidity which is little in keeping with the dynamic and developing nature of our society and our economy." The fact that a law has been passed down from generation to generation does not make it "sound."[109] The forces of technology, economy, and competition and the constantly changing needs of society may in many instances be considered to be more important to the making of law than the precedence of past decisions: "A great deal more innovation in pricing or rate making might be approved if the carrier would only try and propose it . . . it is sometimes the path of least resistance to compete on a basis other than price and place the blame on the regulatory board."[110]

Carriers presently have the opportunity through the ICC's invitation to submit new proposals for cost analysis to be used in rate restructuring proceedings, and ideally should take advantage of this avenue to change the rate structure. The temptation is to restrict change; but

> What some in the industry foresee is not a new technique or device but a realization that loss and damage can play a significant role in rates and operating rights proceedings.
>
> But that day won't come until each carrier and shipper and carrier becomes convinced that loss and damage erodes carrier earnings and increases carrier and shipper costs alike.[111]

NOTES

1. Kenneth U. Flood, Traffic Management (Dubuque, Iowa: Brown, 1975), p. 67.
2. 49 USC 316(b).
3. 49 USC 316(d).
4. 49 USC 316(e).

5. 49 USC 316(g).
6. 49 USC 316(i).
7. Grant M. Davis and Charles S. Sherwood, Rate Bureaus and Antitrust Conflicts in Transportation (New York: Praeger, 1975), Ch. 1.
8. Grant M. Davis and Stephen W. Brown, Logistics Management (Lexington, Mass.: D. C. Heath, 1974), Ch. 11.
9. See Grant M. Davis and Linda J. Combs, "Some Observations Regarding Value of Service Pricing," Transportation Journal (December 1974), pp. 39-59.
10. Ibid.
11. Flood, op. cit., pp. 74, 75.
12. Davis and Brown, op. cit.
13. Richard R. Sigmon, Miller's Law of Freight Loss and Damage Claims, 4th ed. (Dubuque, Iowa: Brown, 1974), p. 332.
14. Ibid.
15. Flood, op. cit., p. 99.
16. Joseph C. Colquitt, The Act and Development of Freight Classification (Washington, D.C.: National Motor Freight Traffic Association, 1956), p. 5.
17. Investigation and Suspension Docket No. M22991, Classification Ratings Based on Density, 337 ICC 786.
18. Rock Island Chamber of Commerce v. Boston & A.R., 148 ICC 63.
19. Colquitt, op. cit., p. 20.
20. Flood, op. cit., p. 100.
21. Flood, op. cit., p. 103, referencing In the Matter of the Suspension of Western Classification No. 51, 25 ICC 442, 788 (1912).
22. Colquitt, op. cit., p. 5.
23. Montgomery Ward & Company v. Abiline & S. Ry. Company, 147 ICC 415.
24. Colquitt, op. cit., p. 16.
25. James C. Harkins, executive director, National Motor Freight Traffic Association, Washington, D.C., telephone conversation, November 2, 1976.
26. Classification Ratings Based on Density, 337 ICC 786.
27. Ibid., 337 ICC 800.
28. Ibid., 337 ICC 806.
29. Colquitt, op. cit., p. 135.
30. A. H. McKinley, "Pinpointing Loss and Damage," Distribution Worldwide, March 1972, pp. 56-60.
31. Flood, op. cit., p. 102.
32. John R. Meyers, Merton J. Peck, John Stenason, and Charles Zwick, The Economics of Competition in the Transportation Industries (Cambridge, Mass.: Harvard University Press, 1969), p. 91.

33. Bruce Whittaker, director of Customer Service, Arkansas Best Freight System, personal interview, October 1976.

34. 337 ICC 786, p. 797.

35. 100 ICC 602.

36. Classification Ratings on Furniture, 177 ICC 5.

37. Colquitt, op. cit., p. 69.

38. Ibid.

39. Dow Chemical Company v. Chesapeake and Ohio Railway Company, et al., 306 ICC 404.

40. Ibid., p. 405.

41. Flood, op. cit., p. 172.

42. Released Rates on Stone in the Southeast, 93 ICC 90 (1924).

43. Ibid.

44. Newton Morton, "Common Law, Common Carriers and Their Transportation of Goods of Extraordinary Value," Paper (Kent, Ohio: Kent State University, 1967), p. 26.

45. Classification Ratings on Clothing, NOI, 349 ICC 237 (1975).

46. Wearing Apparel, Accessories, Piece Goods—Shulman, Inc., 321 ICC 1 (1963).

47. Ibid., pp. 4-5.

48. 349 ICC 237, p. 241.

49. Ibid., p. 206.

50. Released Valuation Rule for Application on All Commodity Rates and Charges on Shipments Weighing Less Than 1,000 Pounds, Mid Atlantic and New England Territories (March 3, 1975).

51. 349 ICC 237, p. 241.

52. Northern Pacific Railway v. North Dakota (236 US 597). Noted in Rail Freight Cost in Various Rate Territories of U.S., Senate Doc. 63, 78th Cong., 1st sess., p. 5.

53. See Davis and Combs, op. cit., pp. 69-85.

54. Docket No. 33597, Talc from Emryville, N.Y., to Ohio, 316 ICC 199 (1962).

55. Investigation and Suspension Docket, No. 7565, Iron and Steel Rings from Pittsburgh, Pa., to Cincinnati, Ohio (1962).

56. Meyers et al., op. cit., p. 64.

57. Ibid.

58. Ibid., p. 91.

59. Ibid., p. 65.

60. Interstate Commerce Commission, Uniform System of Accounts Class I and Class II Common and Contract Motor Carriers of Property (1976).

61. ICC 49 CFR 1207.

62. ICC, Uniform System of Accounts, op. cit., p. 409.

63. Ibid., p. 479.

64. Interstate Commerce Commission, Bureau of Accounts, Terminal Property and Cargo Loss and Damage Expense Allocation, Supplement to Classes I and II Motor Carrier Annual Report Forms for the Cost Study Year 1974, ACC-43 (7/75).

65. Ibid., p. 410.

66. ICC 49 CFR 1207, p. 411.

67. Ibid., p. 436.

68. Ibid., p. 432.

69. Ibid.

70. Ibid., p. 497. For an in-depth examination of motor carrier increases, see Grant M. Davis, Martin T. Farris, and Jack J. Holder, Jr., Management of Transportation Carriers (New York: Praeger, 1975), Ch. 9.

71. ICC 49 CFR 1207, p. 479.

72. Ibid., p. 432.

73. ICC 49 CFR 1005.

74. Ibid.

75. Ibid.

76. Ibid.

77. Ibid.

78. Interstate Commerce Commission, Quarterly Report of Freight Loss and Damage Claims Motor, Schedule A, Loss and Damage Claims Paid Common Carriers of General Freight, Instructions.

79. Ibid.

80. Ibid.

81. Interstate Commerce Commission, Quarterly Freight Loss and Damage Claims (Quarterly), Introductory Statement.

82. Quarterly Report of Freight Loss and Damage Claims, Schedule B, Analysis of Theft, All Carriers, Instructions.

83. Ibid.

84. Form QL&D, Schedule C, Analysis of Claims Processed, All Carriers.

85. Ibid.

86. Ibid.

87. Interstate Commerce Commission, New Procedures in Motor Carrier Revenue Proceedings, Ex Parte No. MC-82, 339 ICC 324.

88. 351 ICC 1.

89. ICC 49 CFR 1104.

90. Ibid., 1104.1(a).

91. Ibid., 1104.1(c).

92. Ibid., 1104.2.

93. Ibid., 1104(b)(1).

94. Ibid., 1104(c)(3).

95. Ibid., 1104(d). The standard errors of some of these samples are rather large.

96. Ibid., 1104.3(a).
97. Ibid., 1104.3(b).
98. Ibid., 1104.3(c).
99. Ibid., 1104.4.
100. Ibid., 1104.6.
101. Ibid., 1104.7.
102. Interstate Commerce Commission, New Procedures in Motor Carrier Restructuring Proceedings Notice of Proposed Rule Making, Ex Parte No. MC-98 (1975), p. 1.
103. Ibid.
104. Ibid., p. 2. For an in-depth examination of carrier subsidies, see Grant M. Davis, Transportation Regulation: A Pragmatic Assessment (Danville, Ill.: Interstate, 1976), Ch. 2.
105. Ex Parte No. MC-98, p. 2.
106. Ibid., p. 4.
107. Ibid.
108. Davis and Combs, op. cit., pp. 89-95.
109. Sigmon, op. cit., p. 5.
110. Davis, Farris, and Holder, op. cit., p. 29.
111. Carlo J. Salzano, "Why Not a Pocketbook Approach to Cargo Loss and Damage," Traffic World, April 7, 1975, p. 29.

4

METHODOLOGY

Primary data employed in this study were collected from a motor truck common carrier of general commodities. The analysis to be performed is dichotomous and includes a study of claims ratio by weight bracket and commodity value information to provide the needed perspective into the motor carrier's liability for goods in general. In this regard, an analysis of cargo value and liability was conducted employing a number of frequency distributions in $1 per pound increments and depicted in tabular form of different amounts of liability ($3, $4, or $5 per pound). An additional objective was to obtain some perspective about the probability of an individual shipment falling into a group of shipments on which claims are experienced. The variables most relevant to predicting a shipment's susceptibility to damage were identified through discriminant analysis. Additional analysis was performed on aggregated data utilizing the variables identified through discriminant analysis in a multiple regression model, with the ultimate intent to construct a reliable predictive model for cargo loss and damage expense of the motor common carrier included in this study.

DATA

Data for the study were available in both computer output form and in manually maintained records from the motor carrier. As much data as possible were gathered in a computer-readable form in an effort to compress the study time frame. The study is subdivided into four major areas: claims ratio by weight bracket, value of shipment analysis, selection of discriminatory variables between claims and no-claims shipments, and the model for predicting cargo loss and damage expense.

Claims Ratio Objectives and Necessary Data

The claims ratio constitutes the principal tool for analysis of claims experience in the motor carrier industry. This is the ratio of claims expense to net revenue. A tabular form of analysis of claims ratio within weight brackets was designed to conform with Ex Parte MC-98.[1] Three variables were necessary for the preparation of the tables: weight of individual shipments in the sample, total revenue, and claims cost. Preparation of the tables was accomplished by aggregation of cases in their respective weight brackets and summing the revenue and claims expense by weight bracket.

Weight and revenue variables were located in the carrier's computer files and were electronically processed. Claims files, on the other hand, are maintained in paper form and therefore were manually processed in order to obtain the needed information. The claims file consists of all pertinent papers to a claims investigation and payment. Documents examined during the study included claims acknowledgment form, freight bill, shipper's invoice, carrier's check copy showing payment of the claim, and carrier's claim investigation report.

A preprinted, prenumbered claims acknowledgment form is written by the computer and serves three major purposes: legal notification to the claimant that a claim has been filed, control of claims through prenumbering, and collection of data in one document of necessary information for reporting to the Interstate Commerce Commission. The form includes most necessary information for reporting as required by law, as well as other information used by the carrier in controlling cargo loss and damage costs. Variables included on the form are claim number, pro number, ICC commodity code, nature of claim code, cause of claim code, traffic type, and the National Motor Freight Classification code. All of this information was obtained during the sampling for present and future study.

Value per Pound Objectives and Necessary Data

Value per pound analyses were designed to include frequency distributions of claims shipments of less than 1,000 pounds in value per pound increments of $1. A similar table that will subsequently be prepared using shipments in all weight categories. Both are designed along the lines of those found in Released Rates Application No. MC-1228.[2] These frequency tables provide a measure of the percentage of shipments in certain value cargo categories, such as $3, $4, or $5 per pound. This partial analysis assists those parties filing applications for released rates and provides the ICC with information for making decisions regarding released rates proposals.

Breakdown tables of value per pound for shipments under 1,000 pounds are also designed to provide a mean value and associated standard deviation by weight bracket. Further analysis includes a breakdown by weight bracket of cost savings associated with shipments released at values of $3, $4, and $5 per pound. This particular information conceivably suggests a blanket value for incorporation in future released rates applications by motor carriers and the ICC. The amount of claims cost savings to be realized at different released valuation amounts was determined in dollar amounts and in percentages in two tables.

Raw data for the analysis of value per pound include shipment weight, value of shipment, the amount of the claim, the total value of the shipment, and a format for the table. Shipment weight was available from the carrier's freight bill in computer-readable form. Value per shipment, together with the amount of claim, is included in the claims record and therefore was extracted manually from the claims file.

An examination of the shipper's invoice in the claims file was undertaken to determine the total value of goods in the shipment. This document was not included in the file for many small claims and in some instances the claimant had furnished only the page of the invoice showing the damaged goods. In this regard, many cases in the sample of claims do not necessarily reflect total value of shipment. Value of the claimed commodity was also ascertained where possible from the shipper's invoice. Obtaining this particular information along with the weight of the claimed commodity was tedious inasmuch as many invoices did not depict unit prices and the manner of packing camouflaged the weight.

The methodology employed for the study of value required designing a data sheet for collection of those data not available in computer-readable form. (The actual design of the data sheet did include some variables that were actually read from a computer input medium.) Data cards were keyed and verified from the form and merged into the appropriate case on the computer output tape.

Discriminant Analysis Objectives and Data

Discriminant analysis was applied to shipment data in order to ascertain a function to compute discriminant scores for the purpose of arriving at an estimate of a shipment's susceptibility to loss or damage. Susceptibility to loss or damage has been established to some degree by the ICC.[3] The National Motor Freight Classification reflects in its class ratings a consideration for a commodity's susceptibility to loss or damage.[4]

The combination of experience and education in the trucking industry certainly provides insight and sensitivity to the factors or variables related to a shipment that contribute to susceptibility to cargo loss or damage. Through the use of discriminant analysis, an attempt is made to identify those variables that most differentiate between "good" and "bad" shipments. Stated differently, the variables that are best discriminators between those shipments likely to fall into a group that will be lost or damaged or more likely to fall into a nonloss or damage group are located.

The two primary research objectives of the discriminant techniques are analysis and classification. In the analysis, various F tests and other statistical tests for measuring how well the discriminating variables actually discriminate are employed. Also, the weighting coefficients serve to identify those variables that are most important in causing differences between the groups.[5] William Klecka utilizes the example of discriminating between Radicals and Liberals in Parliament. In his landmark research, an attempt is undertaken to combine mathematically several political issues so that Radicals would be grouped at one end of a continuum and Liberals at the other end.[6] According to Donald Morrison, one might use the method of discriminant analysis to categorize individuals as good or bad credit risks or potentially good or bad football players:

> A weighted average score is calculated for each of a number of individual objects and on the basis of this score the subject is determined to be a member of one of the groups. The score is based on the independent variables chosen as likely to be the discriminating factors.[7]

Using the football example, Morrison suggests that team officials might use discriminant analysis for the purpose of recruiting. The variables for the study might include speed, weight, and age. "If a particular prospect's variables were weight, 250 lbs.; age, 23; and speed in the forty yard run, 5 seconds, his score would be computed as follows:

$$S = b_1 (250) + b_2 (23) + b_3$$

The numerical score can be transformed into a probability that the individual is a good or bad prospect for the team."[8] In this example, the numerical values of the coefficients b_1, b_2, and b_3 indicate the importance of the independent variables used in the analysis and their ability to discriminate between good and bad prospects.

The two groups to be used in this analysis consist of a group of shipments on which claims have been filed and paid and a second group of shipments on which no claims have been filed. Likely candidates for discriminating variables were intuitively selected on the basis of current knowledge and experience based on interviews with carrier personnel. The discriminant analysis is limited to the information available from the freight bill manifest record. As previously stated, the study carrier maintained a computer file of these records and a number of motor carrier operating variables were extracted therefrom.

For the purposes of this study, the following variables were selected as possible discriminators between the claims group and the no-claims group: class, average weight per piece in shipment, date of shipment, total revenue associated with shipment, total line-haul miles (carried basis), total time of shipment on the trailer, total elapsed time from pickup to delivery to connecting line or consignee, number of times handled, number of pieces in shipment, number of different rates on a bill, traffic type, type packing, originating area, and destination area. For variables such as packing, destination area, and originating area, dummy variables were created. A total of 39 variables were formed from the list, all but one of which were available from the freight bill manifest. Classification rating is the only variable that was not available from an examination of the freight bill manifest information printout. The plan demanded the classification of all 1975 shipments. For this, National Motor Freight Classification NMF 100-C was used.[9]

According to Klecka, in a two-group sample, one discriminant function is formed and consists of the following form:

$$D_i = d_{i1}Z_1 + d_{i2}Z_2 + \ldots + d_{ip}Z_p$$

> where D_i is the score on discriminant function i, the d_i's are weighting coefficients and the Z's are standardized values of the discriminating variables used in the analysis. The weighting coefficients can be interpreted as the weight of a particular variable's contribution to the discriminating function.[10]

The statistical package for the social sciences (SPSS) was employed to select the best set of discriminating variables. Selection was controlled through the use of a stepwise process. Variables were entered into the equation on the basis of Rao's V measure.[11] The concept is to identify the optimum set of discriminating variables.

Discriminant analysis is a classification technique, and in this regard is accomplished through the use of a set of classification functions, one for each group in the study. The classification functions are derived from the discriminant functions and take the form

$$C_i = c_{i1}V_2 + c_{i2} + c_{i2}V_2 + \ldots c_{ip}V_p + c_{io}$$

where C_i is the classification score for the group i calculation, the c_i's are the classification coefficients with c_{io} being the constant, and the V's are the raw scores of the discriminating variables.[12] Applying this to the trucking industry and assuming only three variables, speed, weight, and times handled, the notation is: C_i = the ith shipments' classification score; C_{ij} = the ith classification coefficient of the jth variable; c_{io} = constant; and V_i = the raw score of the ith shipments' discriminating variables. Each shipment would be a linear function of the independent variables, and two classification equations are derived. Assume, moreover, that the equations are as follows:

Group 1 No-Claims $\quad C_i = .01V_1 + .07V_2 + .02V_3$

Group 2 Claims $\quad C_i = .01V_1 + .09V_2 + .3V_3$

If an individual shipment traveled at 50 miles an hour and weighed 200 pounds and was handled six times, these variables would be standardized and entered as follows (assuming standardized values):

Group 1 No-Claims $\quad C_i = (.1 \cdot .20) + (.7 \cdot .50) + (.2 \cdot .3) = .43$

Group 2 Claims $\quad C_i = (.1 \cdot .20) + (.9 \cdot .50) + (.3 \cdot .3) = .56$

In this instance, the higher score is determined when the discriminating variables are entered in the group 2 classification function. This case or shipment would be classified as a case more likely to fall into the claims group than into the no-claims group. After deriving the functions, the SPSS discriminant procedure classifies each case and prints a summary illustrating the number of cases correctly classified.

Regression

Multiple regression analysis may be performed with SPSS, using subprogram regression.[13] Discriminating variables selected through discriminant analysis were used in a regression equation in an attempt to predict claims cost on an aggregate basis. Data necessary for the regression analysis were therefore the same as those used in the discriminant analysis.

SAMPLE DESIGN

In the previous section the variables needed for the study were determined along with their respective location and availability. The remaining steps for completion of the task included a pretest design of the claims data sheet, determination of sample size, selecting the sample, accumulating the data in useful form, and analyzing the results.

Pretest

A total of 7 claims shipments and 26 no-claims shipments were selected as a pretest sample. These cases were selected from data easily obtainable from the carrier and embraced a recent operating period. An attempt was made to simulate as nearly as possible all the conditions expected during the main study. At the same time, additional time studies were conducted to determine the length of time necessary to accomplish the task.

The collection of claims information from the various claims files was time consuming. Although the carrier's files were in excellent condition, the control of claims procedures necessitated collecting correspondence and tracing communications. There was some uniformity in the order of the papers in that the claims acknowledgment followed immediately by the paid check copy was at the front in every file. Because files were stapled together and neatly filed, the selection process itself was accomplished quite easily.

The freight bill numbers from the seven sampled claims shipments were given to the carrier on a form designed by him to facilitate selection of the sample. Claims freight bills as well as the sample of no-claims freight bills were written on computer tape. The tape, supplied by the carrier, was then written out on a new tape in a somewhat modified form that was felt to be more useful. Cards were punched and verified with claims information on the claims shipments and merged into the computer tape, and the resulting data file was punched into cards for the pretesting.

Several forms of the data sheet were designed and employed during the pretest phase. Due to the time necessary to obtain the sample, the design focused upon facilitating the collection of information rather than for the key-punching phase. Some extra care was necessary during the key-punching process, and key punching was verified to help eliminate possible errors. Figure 4 is a sample of the final form of the data sheet.

Data collected on the form included the claim number for control, the pro number, date of shipment, ICC commodity code, nature

FIGURE 4

Sample Data Sheet

DATA FROM CLAIM FILE

CLAIM NUMBER ______ PRO-NUMBER ________ DATE PREPARED ______

ICC COMMODITY CODE ____ NATURE OF CLAIM CODE _ DATE ______

CAUSE TYPE _ TRAFFIC TYPE _ AMOUNT CLAIM __________ TOTAL PIECES ______

NMFC CODE ______ AMOUNT PAID _________ TOTAL WEIGHT SHIPPED ______

TOTAL REVENUE ON BILL _________ CLASS ___ REC _________

CARRIER REVENUE _________

TOTAL PIECES CLAIMED COMMODITY SHIPPED ______ RELEASED VALUATION PER POUND ____ TOTAL WEIGHT CLAIMED COMMODITY SHIPPED ______

REVENUE CLAIMED COMMODITY SHIPPED _________ NO. PIECES CLAIMED COMMODITY CLAIMED ______ WEIGHT OF CLAIMED COMMODITY CLAIMED ______

TOTAL VALUE CLAIMED COMMODITY SHIPPED _________ TOTAL VALUE ALL GOODS SHIPPED _________

GOOD		CTN OR BOX		DRUM		BAG		MISC			
CONGO	_	WDN	_	WDN	_	CLO	_	CRAT	_	KEG	_
INDGO	_	FBD	_	FBR	_	BLP	_	BUND	_	ROL	_
PERIS	_	CGT	_	STL	_	PLP	_	SKID	_	CAN	_
SEHSO	_	OHS	_	ONS	_	ONS	_	BALE	_	ONS	_
								PALL	_		

Source: Standard motor carrier form.

of claims code, date of claim, cause of claim, traffic type, amount of claim, NMFC code, date paid, number of pieces damaged, weight of pieces damaged, released value per pound, total value of shipment, class, and packing information.

An analysis of the time necessary to collect, keypunch, and verify the claims data and to classify 1975 shipments indicated that the sample could not be too large due to time constraints. Thus, a sample size of about 1,400 bills was the maximum that could be handled in the time frame available. Fortunately, a random sample of 1,400 freight bills would not provide enough claim cases for additional value studies to be made. The carrier had calculated that on the average only one out of every 122 shipments results in a filed claim. A projection of the dollar value distribution necessary suggested a sample size of claims shipments of about 280 to 290 claims would provide meaningful value studies. These facts resulted in a decision to select a relatively heavy random sample of claims shipments and a relatively light sample (1,150 to 1,250) of no-claims shipments. Where necessary, weighting was used in the analysis to provide relevant ratios and operating figures. The two groups were classified into two subfiles called no-claims and claims.

The carrier keypunched the freight bill numbers of the claims sample into 80 column data cards and through a computer program took a random start and selected a usable sample of 1,190 no-claims shipments along with the claims bills. This selection process was expected to furnish a sample representative of the traffic handled by the carrier. The freight bill and manifesting data record did not contain any coding to indicate whether or not a claim was filed on a particular shipment. For the purpose of discriminant analysis, a group of exclusively no-claims shipments was needed for comparison of characteristics with a group of exclusively claims shipments. Therefore, it was necessary to list the freight bill numbers of the no-claims subfile and compare these to claims reports of the carrier. Shipments on which claims had been paid were removed, leaving a sample subfile of 1,178 no-claims and a sample subfile of 283 claims.

Eighty column data cards were punched from the data sheets for the claims file information. The computer tapes on which the sample freight bills were merged with the claims data and a modified tape were written. At this point, the analysis phase of the study began, and the data necessary for preparing the tables and performing discriminant and regression analysis were manipulated using the statistical package for the social sciences.

NOTES

1. Interstate Commerce Commission, *New Procedures in Motor Carrier Restructuring Proceedings Notice of Proposed Rule Making, Ex Parte MC-98* (1975), p. 4.

2. Interstate Commerce Commission, *Released Rates Application No. MC-1228, Classification Ratings on Clothing, NOI*, 349 ICC 211 (1975).

3. Interstate Commerce Commission, *Quarterly Freight Loss and Damage Claim Report* (1975).

4. National Motor Freight Traffic Association, *National Motor Freight Classification 100-C* (Washington, D.C.: American Trucking Association, 1976). Also consult Grant M. Davis and Stephen W. Brown, *Logistics Management* (Lexington, Mass.: Heath, 1974).

5. Norman H. Nie et al., eds., *Statistical Package for the Social Sciences* (New York: McGraw-Hill, 1975).

6. William R. Klecka, in *Statistical Package for the Social Sciences*, ed. Norman H. Nie et al. (New York: McGraw-Hill, 1975), p. 435.

7. Donald G. Morrison, "Discriminant Analysis," in *Handbook of Marketing Research*, ed. Robert Ferber (New York: McGraw-Hill, 1974), p. 2-444.

8. Ibid., p. 2-443.

9. National Motor Freight Traffic Association, op. cit.

10. Klecka, op. cit., pp. 435, 436.

11. Nie et al., op. cit., p. 434.

12. Klecka, op. cit., p. 436.

13. Ibid.

5

THE CASE FOR RELEASED RATES

The small shipment problem, illustrated in Chapter 2, if not solved soon may bring about the demise of the regulated segment of the motor carrier industry paralleling the demise of the railroads. Subsidization of high cost traffic through the inflation of profits on low value traffic creates an imbalance in the mix of transportation demand.[1] The motor carrier industry is not isolated from competition, but is besieged on all fronts by other modes of transportation as well as by specialized and private carriers. If a transportation customer can obtain similar service in the movement of goods at a lower cost elsewhere, the motor carrier in turn loses the business.

Two methods of solving the small shipment problem would be to reduce the cost of handling small shipments and to increase the revenue and thus the profit margin on small shipments. The thrust of this analysis will be toward cost reduction in handling small shipments. The analysis will be concentrated in the area of released valuation of goods to limit carrier liability and, to a lesser extent, the simplification of rate structures on small shipments.

The three principal purposes of this analysis are to provide insight into the effect of cargo loss on the cost of operating a common motor carrier of general commodities. The stated goals established at the beginning of the analysis were to estimate motor carrier claims ratios in various weight brackets, compare actual amount of cargo loss and damage expense for shipments under 1,000 pounds in weight with the expense that would have been incurred if those shipments had been made at released rates or ratings, and construct discriminant and regression models for prediction of total cargo loss and damage expense and attempt to measure the susceptibility of an individual shipment to cargo loss and damage.

Information pertinent to the study of cargo loss and damage expense and the development of tables and models was obtained from the claims files, as well as from the freight bill and operating data files maintained by the study carrier. In this regard, the study carrier maintains an extraordinarily sophisticated computerized system for billing purposes. Some manifest information and other relevant operating information such as linehaul miles, trailers used, terminal departure, and receiving times and cube information, are integrated into the freight bill computer file maintained on the company computer.

A random sample of this integrated freight bill and operating data was selected in computer-readable form. The same record was also furnished for each claim sampled, and a relatively large sample of claims was collected along with a more conservative sample of no-claims shipments data. The analysis in some instances includes weighting factors to provide data for estimating such figures as the claims ratio. The tables or other analyses where weighting has been used are appropriately noted.

The various tables will be subsequently presented in order to provide a measure of the value of shipments in value per pound increments of $1 as well as a similar table showing value per pound for shipments in all weight categories. The mean value per pound in various weight brackets may be an important measure and is presented in tabular form. Claims ratio by weight bracket is tabulated and discussed, as well as a presentation showing estimated cost savings that might accrue to the carrier if blanket-released valuation limits were approved for small shipments. Last, a presentation of the results of analysis aimed at predicting the amount of cargo loss and damage expense for a motor carrier of general commodities is given.

VALUE PER POUND

Table 1 reflects a frequency distribution of 96 shipments from the total sample of 283 shipments on which loss or damage claims had been filed. Only shipments of less than 1,000 pounds were selected for inclusion in this table.[2] Indeed, 91.7 percent of shipments weighing less than 1,000 pounds had a value per pound of less than $5, 88.5 percent had a value per pound of less than $4, and 80.2 percent had a value per pound of less than $3. Most proposals for simplified rate structures are accompanied by requests for a blanket-released valuation per pound. Released valuation limits may range from $0.25 percent upward.

The economic significance of the data is in the relatively large number of shipments that would be unaffected by such released valuations. A given motor carrier can absorb loss and damage risk on shipments of relatively low values. However, a problem occurs when the firm handles a high value shipment without knowing the consignment's dollar valuation. Shippers are not required by law

TABLE 1

Frequency Distribution of Claims Shipments
Less than 1,000 Pounds in Value per Pound
Increments of $1

Value per Pound	Number of Shipments	Relative Frequency Percent	Cumulative Percent of Frequency
$ .01 to 0.99	37	38.5	38.5
1.00 to 1.99	35	36.5	75.0
2.00 to 2.99	5	5.2	80.2
3.00 to 3.99	8	8.3	88.5
4.00 to 4.99	3	3.1	91.7
5.00 to 5.99	1	1.0	92.7
6.00 to 6.99	3	3.1	95.8
7.00 to 7.99	0	0	95.8
8.00 to 8.99	1	1.0	96.9
9.00 to 9.99	0	0	96.9
Over 10.00	3	3.1	100.0
Total	96	100.0	

Note: Ninety-six shipments from a group of 283.
Source: Class I General Commodity Motor Carrier Sample.

to divulge the value of goods tendered to carriers for transportation, but must only describe the goods according to instructions in published tariffs. A motor carrier is thus juxtaposed into a position of insuring many shipments without actual knowledge of the extent of financial risk involved. Released valuation limits therefore are designed to limit a carrier's liability to a fixed value so that liability is readily ascertained. Goods that exceed the released valuation figures may be insured by the shipper at full value at increased rates or through employing self-insurance.

As would be expected, where all shipments are included the value per pound increments cluster more closely around the lower values. Larger shipments, when related to weight, may consist of bulky heavy commodities that are exceptionally heavy in relation to their value. When all shipments are included, values per pound tend to be lower than when only shipments of less than 1,000 pounds are considered. In this instance, Table 2 reflects a frequency distribution of value per pound for each shipment in the study for which data were available. Over 92 percent of the shipments in Table 2 show a value per pound of less than $4.

All of the value per pound categories reflect low values when compared to a similar table presented in Classification Ratings on Clothing, NOI.[3] This result is not surprising because clothing can possess a relatively high value when compared with all other goods being transported. In the clothing proceeding available evidence suggests that 88.05 percent of the sampled shipments were valued at less than $8 per pound. As stated above, 88.5 percent of the shipments in this analysis of less than 1,000 pounds had values of less than $4 per pound.

TABLE 2

Frequency Distribution of Claims Shipments of All Weights in Value per Pound Increments of $1

Value per Pound	Number of Shipments	Relative Frequency Percent	Cumulative Frequency Percent
$0.01 to 0.99	103	55.6	55.6
1.00 to 1.99	52	28.1	83.8
2.00 to 2.99	6	3.2	87.0
3.00 to 3.99	10	5.4	92.4
4.00 to 4.99	3	1.6	94.1
5.00 to 5.99	2	1.1	95.1
6.00 to 6.99	4	2.2	97.3
7.00 to 7.99	0	0	0
8.00 to 8.99	1	.5	97.8
9.00 to 19.99	0	0	0
20.00 and over	4	2.2	100.0
Total	185	100.0	

Note: One hundred and eighty-five of 283 sampled claims shipments.

Source: Class I General Commodity Motor Carrier Sample.

In Ex Parte No. MC-98,[4] a framework of weight brackets for consideration in analysis for rate structuring proposals is proposed. The categories are:

	Weight Lbs.
1	Minimum
2	001 - 199
3	200 - 499
4	500 - 999
5	1,000 - 1,999
6	2,000 - 4,999
7	5,000 - 9,999
8	10,000 - Over
9	Total LTL (2 thru 7)
10	Total Minimum and LTL (1 & 9)
11	Truckload (10 & 8)
12	Total All Shipments

An analysis of cost within these weight brackets conceivably can provide information important to the solution of the small shipment problem. A matter of importance to the Interstate Commerce Commission in considering released rate proposals is the value of shipments moving in interstate commerce. The mean value per pound of the entire population of shipments in the sample study was 2.479 with a standard deviation of 2.205.

Table 3 depicts the mean value per pound computations in four weight categories along with the associated standard deviation. If the sample is truly representative of the universe of shipments handled by the study carrier, it is easy to determine that there is a fairly wide range of values in the weight bracket 001 to 199 pounds. The number of shipments in this category is small but the variation may be meaningful. The sum of $22 with a mean of $5.50 per pound and a standard deviation of 4.35 could indicate what might be a relatively high value far to the right of the mean value. The SPSS provides a skewness measure of 2.36 for the frequency distribution of claims shipments under 1,000 pounds value per pound. Skewness measures deviation from symmetry and will take the value of zero when the distribution is a completely symmetric bell-shaped curve. A positive value indicates that most of the cases are clustered to the left of the mean with most of the extreme values to the right.[5] While the sample is small, such analysis using more data cases could prove meaningful.

TABLE 3

Breakdown of Value per Pound for Shipments Under 1,000 Pounds: Claims Filed 18 Months Ending June 1976

Weight (Pounds)	Sum Values per Pound	Mean	Standard Deviation	Number in Group
Minimum	$ 73	2.607	2.283	28
001-199	22	5.50	4.359	4
200-499	100	2.564	2.198	39
500-999	43	1.720	1.10	25
Total	238	2.479	2.205	96

Note: The sample included 96 shipments in the less than 1,000 pound group for which value per pound information was obtainable.

Source: Class I General Commodity Motor Carrier Sample.

CLAIMS RATIOS BY WEIGHT BRACKET

An analysis of claims ratios by weight bracket should provide useful information as to the distribution of claims cost within weight categories. An arrangement of sample data into a table of claims ratios by weight bracket indicates that claims ratios for small shipments are higher than those for shipments weighing over 500 pounds. In this regard Table 4 shows calculations of claims ratios by weight bracket based on weighted data from the sample and a national average claims ratio. The highest claims ratio is 3.50 percent and relates to shipments of 200 to 499 pounds in weight. The next highest ratio was 2.89 percent in the 1 to 199 pound weight bracket, followed by a 2.40 percent claims ratio for minimum shipments. The sum of estimated and weighted revenue figures for the weight categories represented by minimum shipments through 499 pounds is $298,189. The dollar amount of claims paid in these categories sum $9,084. This results in a claims ratio for shipments under 500 pounds of 3.05 percent, a little over three times a national average for all shipments of 1.03 percent.[6] The sum of estimated and weighted revenue figures for the weight categories represented by minimum shipments through

TABLE 4

Claims Ratio by Weight Bracket Based on Overall Claims Ratio of 1.03 Percent and Weighted Revenue Figures, 1975

Line	Shipment Weight	Number of Shipments	Estimated Revenue	Dollar Amount Claims	Claims Ratio Percent
1	Minimum	5,576	$ 105,809	$ 2,536	2.40
2	1-199	754	31,262	905	2.89
3	200-499	4,700	161,118	5,643	3.50
4	500-999	3,096	189,975	2,533	1.33
5	1,000-1,999	2,444	223,641	3,011	1.35
6	2,000-4,999	2,049	307,808	6,416	2.08
7	5,000-9,999	676	201,999	848	.42
8	10,000-Over	1,388	1,183,138	2,998	.25
9	Total LTL (2 through 7)	13,719	1,115,803	19,356	1.73
10	Total minimum and LTL (1 + 9)	19,295	1,221,612	21,892	1.79
11	Truckload (10 + 8)	1,388	1,183,138	2,998	.25
12	Total all shipments	20,683	2,404,750	24,890	1.03

Note: The claims ratio of 1.03 percent is the national average for the quarter ended September 30, 1975. See Interstate Commerce Commission, Quarterly Freight Loss and Damage Claims for the Quarter Ended September 30, 1975 (1975). Revenue distribution is based on allocations from a sample of 973 shipments for the period June 1975 through June 1976. The sample is weighted to provide a claims ratio for comparison purposes of 1.03 percent.

Source: Class I General Commodity Motor Carrier Sample.

999 pounds is $488,164. Total claims sampled in those weighted brackets sum $11,617. These figures yield a weighted claims ratio of 2.38 percent for shipments under 1,000 pounds for the study.

The claims ratio of 3.05 computed for shipments of less than 500 pounds in weight is useful in that it relates to revenue on small shipments. A 1 percent decrease in this ratio is equivalent to adding 1 percent to the year's margin associated with shipments in that category. Such movements in the direction of increased profits through decreased costs on small shipments may result in making such traffic profitable and thereby contribute toward a resolution of the small shipment problem.

COST REDUCTION RELEASED RATES AND SIMPLIFIED BILLING

The small shipment has no exact definition. Most experts would define 500 pounds as a small shipment, but others would allow the weight to be anything under 1,000 pounds.[7] Regardless of the definition, such traffic accounts for a considerable portion of the aggregate traffic handled by the motor carriers. A simplified rate structure based on released rates could contribute greatly toward a solution of the small shipment problem.

Table 5 restates claims ratios for the year 1975 from the sample data. Manipulation of the figures indicates that shipments under 1,000 pounds were 68.30 percent of the total and shipments of less than 500 pounds were 53 percent of total shipments. Of the claims paid 50.56 percent were in the less than 1,000 pounds category and 39.33 percent were in the less than 500 pounds group. As stated earlier in this work and shown in Figure 1, carriers' costs are considerably higher as a percent of revenue for shipments of less than 500 pounds. This is the small shipment problem with which carriers are confronted and for which they may need relief in the form of increased revenue through rate restructuring or in the form of cost reductions. One technique for achieving such a goal might be through the approval of some blanket released rates ordered by the ICC. A substantial number of released rates proposals have been filed over the years, but the commission has exercised its power to grant released rates sparingly. In reviewing cases denying carriers' applications for released rates, an undercurrent of concern about the motor carriers' responsibility for goods is revealed, a concern that may be based on the same reasoning that characterized the development of the common law in England as it applied to common carriers.

Common carriers are required by law to protect goods in their possession as if the goods were the carriers' own property. A car-

TABLE 5

Comparison of Claims Ratios Shipments of Less than 1,000 Pounds and Total Shipments, 1975

	Shipments Less than 500 lbs.	Shipments Less than 1,000 lbs.	All Shipments
Number of shipments	11,030	14,126	20,683
Number of claims	70	90	178
Estimated revenue	$298,189	488,164	2,404,750
Amount of claims	$9,084	11,617	24,890
Claims ratio %	3.05	2.38	1.03

Note: Revenue distribution is based on allocations from a sample of 974 shipments for the period June 1975 through June 1976. The sample is weighted to provide a claims ratio for comparison purposes of 1.03 percent.

Source: Class I General Commodity Motor Carrier Sample.

rier is fully liable to the injured party for any loss or damage occurring while transporting or delivering goods. While the carrier should probably be required by law to protect goods, the argument for unlimited liability may be outdated. Although a select segment of the motor common carrier industry is regulated, there is a relatively high freedom of entry into the market and competition is fierce. An individual motor carrier has nothing to sell but service to customers. That is, one service is to deliver all goods in a salable condition within a reasonable length of time. A loss and damage claim is a loss to all parties concerned, and delays caused by nondelivery or delivery of damaged goods result in lost sales and increased order cost for consignees.

Order filling costs of the shipper will become greater and customers are lost and ill will in general results. When goods are not delivered on time in salable or usable condition, the motor carrier shipper and consignee alike endure economic setbacks. Progressive, well-managed motor carriers use their low claims ratio to obtain and keep customers and a less than average claims ratio is directly related to better customer satisfaction. In fact, the study carrier advertises a low claims ratio in the various transportation journals. A favorable impression is conveyed to present and prospective customers through such advertising and in this regard a sense of pride is created in carrier employees.

The sheer necessity of meeting competition requires that carriers care for and protect goods to the best of their ability. The fear of dishonesty in the common carrier industry today cannot be compared with the fear of dishonesty present when English common law developed. In the U.S. economy as it exists now, rotten apples in a barrel of trucking concerns would soon be found and eliminated through competition. Almost no one would knowingly trade with a dishonest clothier or a dishonest repairman, and few individuals would continue to trade with a laundry and cleaning establishment that returned only a part of his clothing or always returned them in a damaged condition. The argument that carriers would become less responsible for goods under released rates is tenuous because competition provides the necessary stimulus for integrity in the trucking industry today.

Several carriers are authorized by the ICC to accept most goods for shipment under blanket-released rates orders. Examples are the United States Postal Service, United Parcel, and formerly the Railway Express System. The airlines have rates based on released value. A shipper delivering goods to these carriers must release the goods to a maximum value or obtain additional liability coverage through an increased charge. Rates are based on the valuation of the goods and the shipper may recover only that amount equal to or below the amount for which the goods are released. A single 50-pound package may be shipped by United Parcel from Fayetteville, Arkansas 72701, to Meridian, Mississippi 39301, for $6.10. The zip codes are used in the simplified rating system for locating distances. Liability of United Parcel for such a shipment is limited to $100 released valuation, or $2 per pound. Additional insurance is available to the shipper at $0.25 per $100 of coverage which amounts to .25 percent of value premium rate.*

The primary advantage of such a released valuation arrangement is that the carrier may comfortably arrange for shipment of

*Information obtained through toll-free telephone call to United Parcel Service, January 15, 1976.

goods knowing the limits of liability. Should the shipper seek additional insurance the carrier is immediately informed of an increase in the amount of liability and can provide the additional care needed to protect the shipment. The plight of the motor carrier industry today includes the necessity of picking up goods for shipment without knowing the value of the shipment. There is no law requiring the declaration of value by the shipper, and under the present rate structure the carrier is an insurer of goods without knowing the extent of any possible potential loss.

Released rates applications by carriers have proposed limits of liability ranging up to $5 per pound. The Middle Atlantic Traffic Bureau, for instance, has recently filed a released rates application in which small shipments in the less than 500 pounds category would, with the exception of some commodities, be released by the shipper at values not to exceed $100 for any shipment of 100 pounds or less or not exceeding $1 per pound for shipments weighing in excess of 100 pounds.[8] The released rates are a part of a simplified classification and rating proposal that is designed to reduce drastically motor carrier cost affiliated with classifying and rating shipments. The study carrier maintains a sophisticated, smooth, and efficient operation for classifying shipments. Costs are ranging between $0.25 and $0.28 per bill according to the carrier. On the unlikely assumption that most other carriers' costs of classifying and rating freight are so low in amount, such a plan could reduce costs of the motor common carrier industry.[9]

Assume 50 percent of a $0.25 billing cost per shipment could be saved on shipments of less than 500 pounds. The traffic study conducted by the Middlewest Motor Freight Bureau indicates that carriers included in its study handled approximately 64,500,000 minimum LTL and shipments weighing less than 500 pounds. This figure represents 19.5 percent of all traffic handled on a number of shipments basis.[10] Therefore, a savings of 50 percent of an assumed billing cost of $0.25 would amount to 12.5 cents per shipment. The overall effect of such a cost saving could save the U.S. economy for the study carriers alone $8,062,500. The revenue realized on these shipments was approximately $1,091,000,000 and cost savings computed on this basis then would amount to 0.74 percent of the Middlewest Traffic study carriers' revenue on this traffic for the year 1975. The cost saving as a percent of total revenue for 1975 would be 0.14 percent.

Such a cost savings is significant in an industry with overall low profit margins. Insofar as the small shipment problem is concerned, a lowering of billing costs could help increase the differential between cost and revenue, and operating ratios could be reduced. A significant step would be made toward eliminating the small shipment problem and such cost savings could be the basis for rate restructuring proposals aimed at reducing rates on compensative or profitable traffic of the motor carrier. Motor carriers need a method with which to counteract the inroads into their volume made by private carriage, shipper associations, freight forwarders, contract carriage, and illegal trucking. The loss of volume to these competitors is frequently linked to the small shipment problem. That is to say, the cost of operating a tractor and trailer does not differ markedly because of ownership. Indeed, if the motor carrier must charge more in rates for the heavier, more profitable traffic in order to subsidize losses on small shipments, the competitors who can handle such traffic at lower cost will soon divert the traffic.

One objective of this thesis is to provide information about any dollar savings in cost that may be achieved under blanket-released value amounts. During the process of sampling claims records, the value of the shipment was obtained when available. Using this figure and dividing by the weight of the shipment, a dollar per pound valuation was obtained. The difference in these amounts and released value limits of $3, $4, and $5 per pound was found. This provided cost savings that could accrue in the sample through the use of each figure.

Table 6 illustrates claims cost savings by weight brackets using 1975 claims and operating figures. A total of 178 shipments on which some claim had been paid was included in this table. Of the shipment sample, 50.56 percent weighed less than 1,000 pounds and 39.32 percent weighed less than 500 pounds. The total dollar amount of claims for the total of 178 shipments as shown in the table for the year was $24,890. If released valuations of $3 per pound were in effect on these shipments, carrier claims cost would have been decreased by $1,916. If the released value were $4 per pound, the savings in cost would be $1,529, and if the released valuation were $5 per pound, the total claims cost savings would be $1,284—this is in terms of total claims. With respect to only the shipments in the less than 1,000 pounds category, total savings in the released valuation limits of $3, $4, and $5 categories would be $1,716, $1,421, and $1,198, respectively. For shipments under 500 pounds in the $4 category only, the total dollar savings of $1,393 is only 5.60 percent of the total of $24,890 of claims paid. Therefore, if released valuations not to exceed $4 per pound had been in effect during 1975, value exceeding this amount was insured privately by the shipper, and the sample is representative of the universe of claims, the carrier would have saved 5.60 percent of reported claims cost that year.

An examination of minimum and shipments weighing less than 500 pounds in the $4 released value column reveals an interesting relationship. Total claims of $9,084 were expended on shipments

TABLE 6

Reduction of Claims Cost by Weight Bracket Release Value Liability
Not to Exceed $3, $4, and $5, 1975

				Dollar Reduction of Claim Cost		
Line	Shipment Weight	Number of Claims	Dollar Amount of Claims	Released at $3 Pound Value	Released at $4 Pound Value	Released at $5 Pound Value
1	Minimum	28	2,536	188	95	42
2	1-199	4	905	189	145	100
3	200-499	38	5,643	1,299	1,153	1,034
4	500-999	20	2,533	40	28	22
5	1,000-1,999	25	3,011	68	27	16
6	2,000-4,999	24	6,416	47	43	42
7	5,000-9,999	14	848	6	5	4
8	10,000 and over	25	2,998	79	33	24
9	Total LTL (2 through 7)	145	19,356	1,649	1,401	1,218
10	Total minimum and LTL (1 + 9)	153	21,892	1,837	1,496	1,260
11	Truckload (10 + 8)	25	2,998	79	33	24
12	Total all shipments	178	24,890	1,916	1,529	1,284

Source: Class I General Commodity Motor Carrier Sample.

of less than 500 pounds, which is 36.49 percent of the dollar value of all claims filed. Total savings on minimum shipments and shipments weighing less than 500 pounds in the $4 released value category were $1,393. Of the total savings of $1,529 in cost associated with a released valuation not exceeding $4 per pound, 91 percent, or $1,393, is directly attributable to shipments weighing less than 500 pounds. A similar argument can be expanded concerning shipments in the less than 1,000 pounds weight brackets. Thus, while the greatest savings may be realized from small shipments, released valuation would have a small effect percentagewise on the total claims dollars paid by the carrier.

The information in Table 6 is revealing. Claims cost is more significant when related to small shipments under 1,000 pounds or 500 pounds. Released value proposals providing for limited carrier liability on such shipments could provide significant cost savings in an area where an additional differential is needed between revenue and cost. Released rate proposals designed around released valuation and simplified rate structures are techniques that can contribute inordinately to the small shipment problem. Indeed, savings in claims cost coupled with savings in billing cost may be the answer to maintaining a viable common carrier system in the United States.

Claims cost saving expressed as a percent of volume is depicted in Table 7. Cost savings are presented as a percent of revenue by weight bracket in the $3, $4, and $5 categories of released valuation. Those shipments under 500 pounds in Table 6 and in the $4 category, as stated earlier reveal a saving in cost of the sum of $95, $145, and $1,153, or a total of $1,393. Total revenue in all weight brackets from Table 7 is a total of $2,404,750. The cost savings from releasing shipments at values not to exceed $4 per pound in shipment weights of less than 500 pounds would be only 0.05 percent of total revenue, a relatively small percentage and possibly insignificant when viewed in relation to total revenue. The dollar amount is economically significant, however, as a cost reduction on small shipments. Application of this percentage to the total revenue of $5,593,104,242 for the Middlewest study carriers[11] yields a dollar savings of $2,796,552. Again, this is not a large figure when compared to $5.5 billion, but it does constitute a move in the right direction and becomes more significant when perceived in the light of small shipment cost reduction.

An examination of Table 8 provides further insight into the relationship of claims cost to revenue within the less than 500 pounds and less than 1,000 pounds weight brackets. The cost savings from released valuation not to exceed $4 per pound would be .48 percent of revenue associated with minimum and shipments of less than 500 pounds. However, the reduction in the claims ratio in the sample

TABLE 7

Savings in Claims Cost as Percentage Revenue by Weight Bracket Released Value Liability Not to Exceed $3 Pound, $4 Pound, and $5 Pound, 1975

			Percent of Claims Cost Saving to Revenue		
Line	Shipment Weight	Estimated Revenue	Released at $3 Pound Value	Released at $4 Pound Value	Released at $5 Pound Value
1	Minimum	105,809	0.18	0.09	0.04
2	1-199	31,262	0.60	0.46	0.32
3	200-499	161,118	0.80	0.72	0.64
4	500-999	189,975	0.00	0.00	0.00
5	1,000-1,999	223,641	0.03	0.01	0.01
6	2,000-4,999	307,808	0.01	0.01	0.01
7	5,000-9,999	201,999	0.00	0.00	0.00
8	10,000 and over	1,118,138	0.01	0.00	0.00
9	Total LTL (2 through 7)	1,115,805	0.15	0.13	0.11
10	Total minimum and LTL (1 + 9)	1,221,612	0.15	0.12	0.10
11	Truckload (10 + 8)	1,183,138	0.01	0.00	0.00
12	Total all shipments	2,404,750	0.08	0.06	0.05

Source: Class I General Commodity Motor Carrier Sample.

TABLE 8

Comparison of Claims Cost Saving Percent of Shipments of Less than 1,000 Pounds and Total Shipments, 1975 (assuming release valuation $4 per pound)

	Shipments Less than 500 Pounds	Shipments Less than 1,000 Pounds	All Shipments
Number of shipments	11,030	14,126	20,683
Revenue	$289,189	488,164	2,404,750
Cost saving released at $4 pound	1,393	1,421	1,529
Claims cost saving as percent of revenue	0.48	0.29	0.06

Note: Revenue distribution is based on allocations from a sample of 974 shipments for the period June 1975 through June 1976. The sample is weighted to provide a claims ratio for comparison purposes of 1.03 percent.

Source: Class I General Commodity Motor Carrier Sample.

study for the year 1975 would have been only .057 percent. If the released valuation not exceeding $4 per pound applied to all minimum shipments and shipments weighing less than 1,000 pounds, the claims cost would have been reduced by 0.29 percent of the revenue applicable to this division of business, and the savings in total claims ratio would be .059 percent. Savings in claims cost would be small when viewed as a percentage of total revenue, but such savings would be quite large when viewed as a total of revenue within weight brackets. Due to the nature of the distribution of claims within weight brackets, a released value rate structure plan would tend to match any claims cost savings with its associated revenue. Such a plan would appear to be a direct means of attacking the small shipment problem and thereby helping to preserve the common carrier system, which is so essential to the economic foundation of the United States. Economic regulation of the common carrier actually requires that the firm provide service to all within the scope of its operating authority. If this system is to be preserved, motor carriers should be allowed to price services in accordance with the cost of such services. As with any business, profits are necessary to healthy survival in the long run. But if competition takes the profitable traffic and leaves the unprofitable traffic for the motor carrier, another important segment of the transportation system may follow the railroads to disaster.

COMMODITY GROUPS AND CLAIMS

During the data-gathering phase of this study, the ICC commodity code of goods affected in a claims payment was recorded. A frequency distribution of these commodity codes along with the associated dollar amount of claims and the claims cost saving in three categories of released valuation limits is shown in Table 9. Because this analysis deals with a study carrier whose claims ratio is considerably below the national average (for the past three years it has not exceeded 0.50 percent), this distribution should provide some measure of a code group's susceptibility to loss or damage from factors other than handling.

ICC code group 2500 bears the description furniture and fixtures. For the entire 18-month sample, 28 claims were paid on this commodity group with a claims cost totaling $2,183. Savings in claims expense realized from released valuation in this group would be 0.28 percent at the $3 limit, 0.09 percent at the $4 limit, and 0 percent at the $5 limit. A number of commodity groups were involved in claims payments from 11 to 28 times each in the sample. The numbers of these groups and their related descriptions excluding code 4600, miscellaneous freight shipments NOI, are as follows:

Code No.	No. Claims	Commodity Description
2000	14	Food or allied products
2030	13	Food, canned, dried, preserved, pickled
2500	28	Furniture and fixtures
2840	12	Soaps, detergents, and cleaning compounds
2850	11	Paints, varnishes, enamels, lacquers
3000	16	Plastics and rubber products NOI
3400	13	Metal products, fabricated NOI
3420	13	Hardware except power tools
3640	11	Lamps, shades, electric lighting equipment, parts
Total	131	

A total of nine commodity groups then accounted for 131 of 283 claims sampled. Stated somewhat differently, approximately 20 percent of the commodity groups accounted for 46 percent of the claims paid. Claims cost for these commodities amounted to $10,573 for the sample, or 28.48 percent of total dollar amount of claims paid for the entire sample.

About one fourth of the commodity groups accounted for 72 percent of the total dollar value of claims. The group numbers and their descriptions follow:

Code No.	Amount	Description
2200	$ 1,122	Textiles, woven knit, miscellaneous, mill products NOI
2300	4,249	Clothing except fur and fur trimmed
2500	2,183	Furniture and fixtures
2600	1,254	Paper and paper products
2840	2,397	Soaps, detergents, and cleaning compounds
2850	2,128	Paints, varnishes, enamels, lacquers
3000	1,937	Plastic and rubber products, NOI
3210	1,068	Glass, flat or bent
3400	1,162	Metal products, fabricated NOI
3420	1,033	Hardware except power tools
3430	5,980	Plumbing and heating fixtures, supplies
3600	2,067	Electrical machinery, equipment, supplies NOI
Total	$26,580	
Total, all claims	$37,124	

Again, selecting the $4 per pound released valuation limit for analysis, 20 of the total of 44 commodity groups sampled would contribute to claims cost savings were a released value proposal in effect at that value. The claims cost saving for this group would amount to 7.26 percent of total claims paid. At the $5 limit only 15 commodity groups would contribute to cost savings and 5.84 percent of the total claims cost would be realized. Admittedly, this sample is not of a magnitude to provide a distribution of all the 63 commodity groups reported by the ICC. However, the sample may be representative of the study carrier's traffic. If this is true, only a few of the commodity groupings would provide significant savings in claims cost. At the $4 per pound limit, for instance, commodity 2300, clothing except fur and fur trimmed, and commodity 3600, electrical machinery, equipment, supplies, NOI, demonstrate a cost savings of $1,048 and $1,068, respectively (see Table 9).

These figures represent 25 and 76 percent of the original claims amount. In terms of absolute dollar amounts, under a $4 released

TABLE 9

Claims and Reduction of Claims Cost by Interstate Commerce Commission Commodity Codes, Shipments of Less than 1,000 Pounds, January 1, 1975 Through June 1976

			Dollar Savings Claims Cost		
ICC Code	Total Number of Claims	Dollar Amount of Claims	Released at $3 Pound Value	Released at $4 Pound Value	Released at $5 Pound Value
0842	1	$ 36	0	0	0
1900	2	442	27	0	0
2000	14	690	0	0	0
2030	13	442	51	8	0
2037	1	33	29	26	24
2042	1	81	0	0	0
2050	5	360	0	0	0
2070	7	335	0	0	0
2080	2	40	0	0	0
2110	1	12	0	0	0
2200	2	1,122	21	0	0
2270	8	466	1	0	0
2300	6	4,249	1,405	1,048	754
2390	3	300	142	102	62
2500	28	2,183	8	2	0
2600	9	1,254	0	0	0
2700	1	25	0	0	0
2800	6	311	3	0	0
2830	3	255	2	1	0

2840	12	2,397	0	0	0
2844	9	151	0	0	0
2850	11	2,128	44	43	42
2870	2	17	0	0	0
3000	16	1,937	13	10	7
3010	3	562	0	0	0
3200	6	398	4	0	0
3210	4	1,068	2	0	0
3220	9	217	51	41	33
3300	4	411	0	0	0
3400	13	1,162	0	0	0
3420	13	1,033	24	7	0
3430	6	5,980	20	19	18
3500	5	810	0	0	0
3520	3	516	60	27	22
3540	1	45	0	0	0
3600	6	2,067	1,168	1,068	968
3630	5	212	96	78	74
3640	11	998	97	57	38
3650	1	3	1	0	0
3652	1	54	6	1	0
3714	3	205	0	0	0
3910	1	83	54	44	34
3940	9	319	75	61	50
4600	11	1,399	38	6	4
Missing	4	306	54	49	38
Total	283	$37,124	$3,495	$2,698	$2,168

Source: Class I General Commodity Motor Carrier Sample.

valuation limit, these two commodities account for 78.43 percent of total claims cost savings. This fact suggests that these two groups are somewhat higher in value on the average than other commodity groups. Of course, an individual may purchase a suit of clothes at retail prices ranging from $50 to over $500. A particular piece of machinery may have elaborate engineering requirements, making its value many times as much as another piece of machinery not requiring any great technology of manufacturer. A wide range of value exists within these two commodity code groups, making the amount of any claim difficult to predict. Certainly there is a possibility of excessive discrimination when goods of high value can move with full liability coverage, while other similar goods with low value must move at the same rate. A rate restructuring plan with a limitation of liability and a provision for additional liability coverage available at extra cost for values exceeding the limitation may be more equitable for the shipping public as a whole.

A brief summary of the estimated cost savings accruing to the sample study carrier is in order. On the assumption that one half of the billing cost could be saved on shipments of less than 500 pounds through some simplified rating plan, a cost savings of 0.14 percent of revenue could be realized. Adding this to savings of approximately 0.05 percent in claims paid provides a total saving of 0.19 percent. This may be shown as follows:

Claims cost saving—released valuation at $4 per pound	.05%
Billing cost saving—simplified rate structure	.14%
Total savings as a percent of total revenue	.19%

Subtracting the .05 percent from the national average claims ratio of 1.03 percent for the quarter ended September 30, 1975 would provide a claims ratio of .98 percent and this cost reduction would apply to small shipments under 500 pounds, as would the .14 percent billing cost saving.

Although the savings in claims cost are significant, it is interesting to observe again from Table 1 that 80.2 percent of the shipments represented by the sampled claims had values per pound of less than $3, 88 percent had values per pound of less than $4, and 91.7 percent had value per pound of less than $5. The sample is small and may not be representative of the whole. However, the figures provide some indication of the impact that released values can have on carrier liability. Assuming these figures are representative, the motor carrier would remain liable for the full value of most shipments. Those shippers whose products exceed a released valuation ceiling could obtain full coverage if desired through additional charges by the motor carrier, purchase marine insurance, or elect to have the goods move at the released value. Most shippers of drug and toilet preparations ship goods at released valuation not to exceed $0.50 per pound and either self-insure or purchase insurance to cover losses in excess of this limitation. Most shippers should be able to establish values of shipments within a very close range for the purpose of declaring values for additional coverage where wanted.

DISCRIMINANT ANALYSIS

Through the use of subprogram discriminant of the SPSS, a set of discriminating variables was selected to differentiate between no-claims and claims shipments. Two research techniques are available through the use of this program: analysis and classification. From an analysis standpoint, the procedure is used in this thesis to locate those variables that contribute most to the separation of the no-claims and claims groups. The standardized discriminant function coefficients of the X_i variables in the discriminant function provide a means for evaluating any variable's relative contribution as a differentiator between the groups.

The classification application of the program is employed to classify the cases on the basis of group membership. A measure of the ability of the discriminating function to discriminate between the groups is thus obtained by calculating the percentage of shipments correctly classified.

Cases for this study were composed of the random sample of 1975 shipments. There were 471 no-claims shipments and 170 claims shipments in this group. Shipments in the no-claims group were classified using National Motor Freight Classification 100-C. The remaining information was obtained from a computer tape furnished by the carrier and on which the random sample of data was recorded.

The following variables were selected on the basis of judgment as possible discriminators between the two groups. Judgment was made on the basis of current knowledge and experience based on interviews with carrier personnel and all variables with the exception of class were available in computer-readable form for most shipments: class, average weight per piece in the shipment, date of shipment, carrier revenue associated with the shipment, linehaul miles (carried basis), total time on trailer (carried basis), total lapsed time from pickup to delivery to connecting line or consignee, number of times handled, number of pieces in shipment, number of different rates on bill, traffic type, type packing (dummy variables used here), originating area (dummy variables used here), and destination area (dummy variables used here).

Dummy variables were created for packing with a value of 0 or 1. The types of packing variables were carton or box, fiber box, fiber drum, steel drum, bag, crate, bundle, skid, bale, pallet, roll, and case. Also, dummy variables with a value of 0 or 1 were created for the geographical areas used by the carrier for its own revenue cost analysis. A set of variables was created for both originating area and destination area. The date of shipment was assigned weights corresponding to the national average claims ratio as reported by the Interstate Commerce Commission. These were for the consecutive quarters ending March 31, 1975, 1.32 percent; June 30, 1975, 1.20 percent; September 30, 1975, 1.03 percent; December 31, 1975, 1.13 percent.

A stepwise procedure was employed to eliminate those variables found not to be good discriminators. SPSS provides for the use of five different methods for stepwise selection of discriminating variables. Rao's V is a generalized distance measure where variables are added to the function on the basis of the amount of increase in this distance V. The variables not in the equation are tested simply in conjunction with the set of variables already contained in the equation. That variable contributing toward the largest increase in Rao's V when considered with the previous variables chosen is added to the equation.

According to William Klecka this amounts to the greatest overall separation of the groups. A change "in V has a chi square distribution with one degree of freedom so it can be tested for statistical significance."[12] Along with this criterion, subprogram discriminant will consider selecting a variable "only if its partial multivariate F ratio is larger than a specified value. This test is made by the program before the Rao's V criteria was applied." A small partial F would eliminate the variable from consideration and a variable may be removed from the equation during the stepwise selection process if its removal and replacement by another variable would add to the discriminating ability of the function. The partial F must be smaller than a specified value supplied by the user before a variable would be deleted from the equation. In this study the partial F default value of 1.000 was used for inclusion of a variable and the partial F default value of 1.000 was used for removal of a variable. These default values are low enough so that a variable with almost any discriminating characteristic would be included in the resulting discriminant function.[13] Further research might be conducted for the purpose of increasing somewhat the value of F for a more rigorous test before entrance of a variable into the equation.

A maximum of 96 steps could be performed by the discriminant program in use during the study. A total of 22 steps was performed before reaching an F level insufficient for further computation. Table

10 is derived from the computer summary printout of the 22 variables selected as the best discriminators between the no-claims and claims groups. The class of the shipment was found to be the best discriminator between the groups, with a final F to remove of 29.36212 and a Wilkes lambda of .95607. Wilkes lambda is a measure of the function's discriminating value. The larger the Wilkes lambda, the less discriminating power. Lambda does decrease as variables are added to the equation, however, the final value of .81494 may seem high; but the chi square indicates that a statistically significant amount of discriminatory power exists in the chosen variables. The printout depicts a significance of 0.0000, thus lambda is significant at least at the .01 level. The increasing value of lambda at each step indicates that discriminating power is being added to the function through the addition of new variables. After selecting 22 of the 48 variables, the change in Rao's V was significant at the .225 level and the selection was ended by the program. The reader should notice that relatively large changes in Rao's V occur upon entry of the first two variables, class and total pieces.

The changes in Rao's V are significant at the 10 percent level through step 16, after which the changes are less significant. Further manipulation and experimentation with the data might turn up a discriminating function with less variables. In this study, however, all variables with discriminating power as measured by the partial F default value of 1 were selected, and will be used in multiple regression analysis in an attempt to develop a model for predicting the amount of cargo loss and damage expense for the motor carrier being examined.

As shown earlier, the discriminant function takes the form

$$D_i = d_{i1}Z_1 + d_{i2}Z_2 + \ldots d_{ip}Z_p$$

where D_i is the score on discriminant function i, the d_i's are weighting coefficients, and the Z's are the standardized values of the p discriminating variables used in the analysis. The standardized discriminant function coefficients computed by the program are listed in Table 11.

The reader should notice that the constant is not in the equation when the coefficients are standardized. These standardized coefficients correspond to the d_i's. A discriminant score may be computed using these coefficients and the 22 variables in standardized form in the equation. A discriminant score will be computed for each case. Over all the cases in the analysis the scores will have a mean of 0 and a standard deviation of 1. A single score represents the number of standard deviations that a particular case is away from the mean of all cases. The absolute values of the standardized discriminant

TABLE 10

Discriminating Variables Selected by Discriminant Analysis: Cargo Loss and Damage Study, 1975

Step Number	Variable Entered	Variable Removed	F to Enter or Remove	Wilkes Lambda	Sig.	Rao's V	Change in Rao's V	Sig. of Change
1	Class		29.36212	0.95697	0.000	29.36273	29.36273	0.000
2	Total pieces		23.54666	0.92204	0.000	54.02985	24.66711	0.000
3	Number classes		8.43837	0.90998	0.000	63.21175	9.18190	0.002
4	Carton or box		8.71463	0.89768	0.000	72.83357	9.62183	0.002
5	Times handled		7.35529	0.88740	0.000	81.07837	8.24480	0.004
6	Destination area no. 7		6.91524	0.87783	0.000	88.93311	7.85474	0.005
7	Date of shipment		8.02926	0.86683	0.000	93.01294	4.07983	0.043
8	Pallet		3.07623	0.86264	0.000	96.57819	3.56525	0.059
9	Total weight		4.78075	0.85615	0.000	102.16608	5.58789	0.018
10	Carrier revenue		4.64132	0.84989	0.000	107.61816	5.45209	0.020
11	Average weight per piece		3.57668	0.84508	0.000	111.86276	4.24460	0.039
12	Fiber box		2.98383	0.84109	0.000	115.40952	3.54675	0.060
13	Rate		3.21793	0.83679	0.000	119.27341	3.86389	0.049
14	Originating area no. 8		2.52077	0.83343	0.000	122.32901	3.05560	0.080
15	Can		2.89556	0.82959	0.000	125.85217	3.52316	0.061
16	Destination area no. 10		2.28019	0.82657	0.000	128.61429	2.76212	0.097
17	Originating area no. 6		2.11329	0.82377	0.000	131.21915	2.60486	0.107
18	Originating area no. 9		1.84516	0.82134	0.000	133.49220	2.27306	0.132
19	Originating area no. 4		1.41303	0.81947	0.000	135.24890	1.75670	0.185
20	Traffic type		1.17451	0.81792	0.000	136.63219	1.38329	0.240
21	Skid		1.08798	0.81649	0.000	137.98532	1.35313	0.245
22	Crate		1.17397	0.81494	0.000	139.45926	1.47394	0.225

Source: Compiled by the authors.

TABLE 11

Discriminant Function Coefficients

Variable		Standardized	Unstandardized
Z_1	Average weight	-0.16905	-0.00009
Z_2	Date of shipment	-0.15567	-1.51877
Z_3	Carrier revenue	-0.43430	-0.00162
Z_4	Times handled	-0.40372	-0.15970
Z_5	Total pieces	0.37155	0.00089
Z_6	Total weight	0.58654	0.04256
Z_7	Rate	0.17558	0.03787
Z_8	Number classes	0.21814	0.21245
Z_9	Traffic type	0.14428	0.17114
Z_{10}	Class	0.49589	0.01163
Z_{11}	Carton or box	-0.33866	-0.68467
Z_{12}	Fiber box	-0.16506	-1.58699
Z_{13}	Crate	-0.09416	-0.90528
Z_{14}	Skid	-0.09882	-0.43459
Z_{15}	Pallet	-0.20480	-0.95391
Z_{16}	Can	0.14318	1.62629
Z_{17}	Originating area no. 4	-0.12074	-0.49305
Z_{18}	Originating area no. 8	-0.18449	-0.46388
Z_{19}	Originating area no. 10	-0.13103	-1.66262
Z_{20}	Destination area no. 7	-0.28185	-0.82632
Z_{21}	Destination area no. 9	-0.09865	-0.46671
Z_{22}	Destination area no. 10	-0.15468	-1.60503
	Constant		2.08457

Source: Compiled by the authors.

function coefficients are a measure of its corresponding variable's contribution to the discriminating function. A review of Table 11 illustrates that total weight of the shipment with a standardized coefficient of .58 is the most important discriminating variable. Total weight is followed in order of decreasing importance by class, 0.49; carrier revenue, 0.43; times handled, 0.40; total pieces, 0.37; and so on.

The unstandardized coefficients do not provide any measure of a variable's contribution to the function's discriminating power but do provide a means of calculating a discriminant score when the variables are not standardized in the equation. By calculating a discriminant score for each case in the two groups and plotting them on a continuum, one may visually observe the clustering of cases around the mean of each group, as illustrated in Figure 5.

The zero point on this continuum is the general mean of all the cases, both no-claims and claims. The group centroid is the mean score for that group. While the separation may not be large between the groups, nevertheless there is separation. Classification of the cases using the classification functions provides an indication of the success of the function in discriminating between the two groups.

The classification functions are derived from the discriminating function. In a two-group sample, two classification functions are derived, one for each group. The equations are applied to each case giving two probabilities. If the probability computed from the no-claims group classification function exceeds the probability computed using the claims group classification function, the case is assigned as a member of the no-claims group of cases and vice versa. The classification functions take the form

$$C_i = c_{i1}V_1 + c_{i2}V_2 + \ldots c_{ip}V_p + c_{io}$$

where C_i is the classification score for group i, the C_{ip}'s are the classification coefficients with c_{io} being the constant, and the V's are the raw scores on the discriminating variables.

The classification function coefficients for group 1, no-claims shipments, and for group 2, claims shipments, are listed in Table 12.

Discriminant scores and classification probabilities were computed for each case in the study. The actual group membership is known for all the cases because of the method of selecting the sample and the subfile structure of the data set. Each case was listed in the form as shown in Table 13.

Table 13 is a condensation of the actual printout illustrating the results of the classification phase of this study. Shown for each case is its subfile membership, case number, actual group membership, misclassification code, the group scoring the highest probability of membership, the group scoring the next highest probability of membership, and the case's discriminant score. The actual group membership for the first ten cases is group 1, no-claims. If the highest group probability is scored by the classification function releated to the no-claims group, a correct classification results, that is, the characteristics of the variables applicable are truly those of a no-claims case as defined by the discriminant function and the shipment did not result in a claim. In the event that actual group membership is no-claims and the highest probability is scored

FIGURE 5

Territorial Map of
Discriminant Score 1 (Horizontal)
Versus Discriminant Score 2 (Vertical)

```
           -3.000                   -1.500                  0.0                    1.500                    3.000
             + --------- + ---------- + --------- + --------- + ---------- +----------+ -----------+ ----------- +
  3.000  I                                                                                                       I
         I                                                                                                       I
         I                                                                                                       I
         I                                                                                                       I
         I                                                                                                       I
  2.250  I                                                                                                       I
         I                                                                                                       I
         I                                                                                                       I
         I                                                                                                       I
  1.500  I                                                                                                       I
         I                                                                                                       I
         I                                                                                                       I
         I                                                                                                       I
  0.750  I                                                                                                       I
         I                                                                                                       I
         I                                                                                                       I
         I                                                                                                       I
         I                                                                                                       I
  0.0    I 111111111111111111111111111111111111111111111*11111122222222*22222222222222222222222222222222222222 I
         I                                                                                                       I
         I                                                                                                       I
         I                                                                                                       I
         I                                                                                                       I
 -0.750  I                                                                                                       I
         I                                                                                                       I
         I                                                                                                       I
         I                                                                                                       I
 -1.500  I                                                                                                       I
         I                                                                                                       I
         I                                                                                                       I
         I                                                                                                       I
 -2.250  I                                                                                                       I
         I                                                                                                       I
         I                                                                                                       I
         I                                                                                                       I
         I                                                                                                       I
 -3.000  I                                                                                                       I
             +---------- +---------- +---------- + --------- +---------- +----------+-----------+----------- +
```

Source: Constructed by the authors.

TABLE 12

Classification Function Coefficients

		Group 1 No-Claims	Group 2 Claims
V_1	Average weight	0.00040	0.00030
V_2	Date of shipment	117.75151	116.04593
V_3	Carrier revenue	0.00460	0.00272
V_4	Times handled	2.90950	2.72417
V_5	Total pieces	0.00133	0.00236
V_6	Total weight	0.00650	0.05612
V_7	Rate	0.08624	0.13047
V_8	Number classes	0.78196	1.02991
V_9	Traffic type	-4.11846	-3.92046
V_{10}	Class	0.02153	0.03510
V_{11}	Carton or box	3.13928	2.34137
V_{12}	Fiber box	-5.90008	-7.75578
V_{13}	Crate	-0.20238	-1.25988
V_{14}	Skid	5.22908	4.72375
V_{15}	Pallet	2.91938	1.80722
V_{16}	Can	3.37484	5.27388
V_{17}	Originating area no. 4	0.56529	-0.00974
V_{18}	Originating area no. 8	0.31938	-0.22218
V_{19}	Originating area no. 10	4.42760	2.48842
V_{20}	Destination area no. 7	2.72817	1.76473
V_{21}	Destination area no. 9	-2.50713	-3.05346
V_{22}	Destination area no. 10	11.51915	9.65224
	Constant	-82.01187	-79.92741

Source: Class I General Commodity Motor Carrier Sample.

by the classification function related to the claims group, four asterisks are printed showing that the characteristics of that shipment's variables would place it in the claims group of shipments. Each individual case was listed in the printout. The ability of the discriminating variables to differentiate between the two groups was fair and is shown in Table 14.

The sample size is small compared to the great number of shipments handled by the carrier in the study. The ratio of claims

TABLE 13

Discriminant Classification of No-Claims and Claims Shipments, 1975

Subfile	Case No.	Actual Group	Misclassification (****)	Highest Probability		Next Highest Probability		Discriminant Scores
				Group	P(G/X)	Group	(PG/X)	
No-claim	1	1		1	0.697	2	0.303	-0.490
No-claim	2	1	****	2	0.526	1	0.474	0.316
No-claim	3	1		1	0.549	2	0.451	0.055
No-claim	4	1		1	0.587	2	0.413	-0.078
No-claim	5	1		1	0.857	2	0.143	-1.311
No-claim	6	1		1	0.684	2	0.316	-0.436
No-claim	7	1		1	0.625	2	0.375	-0.212
No-claim	8	1	****	2	0.648	1	0.352	0.749
No-claim	9	1		1	0.750	2	0.250	-0.719
No-claim	10	1		1	0.514	2	0.486	0.175
Claim	1	2		2	0.869	1	0.131	1.849
Claim	2	2		2	0.574	1	0.426	0.479
Claim	3	2	****	1	0.662	2	0.338	-0.352
Claim	4	2		2	0.858	1	0.142	1.769
Claim	5	2		2	0.546	1	0.454	0.383
Claim	6	2	****	1	0.687	2	0.313	-0.448
Claim	7	2		2	0.928	1	0.072	2.414
Claim	8	2		2	0.926	1	0.074	2.394
Claim	9	2		2	0.745	1	0.255	1.143
Claim	10	2	****	1	0.520	2	0.480	1.157

Source: Class I General Commodity Motor Carrier Sample.

TABLE 14

Cargo Loss and Damage Study Prediction of Group Membership Classification of Cases Using Discriminant Classification Function

	Group 1 No-Claims	Group 2 Claims
No. of cases	471	170
Predicted group membership		
Group 1		
Total	347	124
Percent	73.7	26.3
Group 2		
Total	60	110
Percent	35.3	64.7

Percent of cases correctly classified: 71.29 percent.
Source: Class I General Commodity Motor Carrier Sample.

shipments to no-claims shipments in the sample is about 1 to 4; and the actual claims shipment to no-claims shipments ratio of the carrier is about 1 to 122. Also, additional study after the discriminant analysis suggests that traffic type might be better entered into the analysis as a 0 or 1 dummy variable instead of in weighted amounts of 1 to 4. Information to supply the amounts of some of the variables was not available in early 1975 records when the computer application to record manifest and bill data was not available. In view of this, some of the cases did not have sufficient data for calculation of the estimated number of times a shipment was handled and the destination and originating areas. Even with these shortcomings the study does indicate that discriminant analysis may be a helpful management tool in directing the cargo loss and damage prevention programs a general commodity motor carrier should have. Additionally, discriminant analysis is helpful in selecting possible variables for subsequent use in multiple regression analysis.

The discriminant function appears to predict more successfully actual group membership for the no-claims shipments. Three hundred and forty-seven, or 73.7 percent, of the no-claims scored the highest probability on their own classification function. The claims group of shipments was not so easily predicted inasmuch as only 64.7 percent of claims shipments were correctly classified. Some encouragement, however, may be found in the fact that 71.29 percent of all shipments were correctly classified as to group membership. Misclassification of 28.71 percent of shipments is, nevertheless, a large margin for error.

The application of discriminant analysis to the data in this study does serve to isolate those variables that differentiate between shipments on which no claims are paid and those on which a liability is realized and paid. Again, the standardized discriminant function coefficients reveal that total weight is the discriminator of most importance in differentiating between potentially claims shipments and no-claims shipments. The size and magnitude of the d_i's determine the effect of the independent variables. Logically, the larger the coefficient, the larger the product when it is multiplied by the variable Z_i. The direction of the effect on the discriminant score is shown by the sign of d_i. If the sign is positive, the discriminant score will be influenced in a positive direction; conversely, if the sign is negative, the score will move in a negative direction.

In this discriminant function, positive scores suggest membership in the claims group of shipments, while negative scores suggest membership in the no-claims group. Therefore, an examination of the variable Z_1, average weight per piece, shows a standardized discriminant function coefficient of -0.16905. The effect of an increase in the average weight of a shipment, then, would be to move the discriminant score toward the no-claims group of shipments. The lower the average weight per piece in the shipment, the less influence this negative weight would have and the scores would be more likely to be positive, placing the shipment into the claims group. Class, on the other hand, has a positive standardized discriminant function coefficient of 0.49589, thereby making a positive contribution toward the discriminant score. Shipments in the higher class brackets are more susceptible to loss and damage, as the higher the class the greater the positive direction of the discriminant score. Intuitively, this must be true since one criterion for establishing class ratings is an individual commodity's susceptibility to loss and damage.

Originating areas 4, 8, and 10 and destination areas 7, 9, and 10 make a negative contribution to the discriminant function score. The influence of any one variable also must be considered in light of all variables in the function. It is therefore difficult to interpret the significance of these coefficients except to say that a negative influence might be expected if a particular area has a particularly low incidence of claims. According to Bruce Whittaker,[14] freight moving into a particular destination area may be mostly backhaul freight that may not be susceptible to cargo loss or damage or such shipments are large and carry only one freight bill rather than several freight bills representing several shipments. The probability of damage occurring in a load consisting of several shipments is greater than in a single shipment load.

The influence of originating and destination areas in the equation is difficult to assess because several terminals may be located in one area. Even though the terminal in an area may have an excellent claims experience, another terminal in the same area may have a fairly high incidence of claims. Discriminant analysis must combine the experience factors of all terminals located in an area in determining the sign and amount of that area's coefficient. Further research into the influence of geographical location in discriminant analysis of cargo loss and damage experience is certainly needed. A more forthright approach might be an analysis using individual terminals as variables. This could be a strong tool for management in bringing together the factors influencing a specific terminal's claims record.

Test of the Function

The discriminant function has been fitted to the particular set of data gathered in the study and the group of claims shipments does not represent a true proportion of claims shipments and no-claims shipments. Thus the use of the discriminant analysis to identify shipments likely to result in claims is confounded by the reality that the prior probability of a claim is only .0081 for the study carrier. For the sake of discussion, assume this prior probability is .01. A shipment, then, has a prior probability of being a no-claims shipment. In classifying a shipment as a claims shipment, one is "bucking the pure chance odds."[15]

Following the reasoning of William Morrison, let the proportion of the population that is related to claims shipments equal p and the proportion that is related to no-claims equal 1 - p. If the variables in the function are not discriminators, one could reasonably expect to obtain a proportion p correctly classified if every shipment is classified as no-claims. If $p < \frac{1}{2}$, all shipments could be classified as no-claims and better than 50 percent could be predicted correctly.

The pure chance proportion correctly classified if 1 percent of shipments were classified as claims would be as follows: Let p be the true proportion of claims shipments; a, the proportion classified as claims shipments; $p\ (\text{correct}) = pa + (1 - p)(1 - a)$; $p = .01$; $a = .01$; $p = (.01)^2 + (.99)^2 = .9802$. The chance proportion correctly classified would be 98.02 percent. The maximum chance criterion would be represented by

$$C_{max} = \max(a,\ 1 - a)$$

when max(a, 1 - a) is read, the larger of a or 1 - a. In our case, max(0.01, 0.99) = .99. If the discriminating function can do no better than C_{max}, it is better to disregard it and merely classify every one as belonging to the larger of the two groups.

As mentioned earlier, a relatively large sample of claims shipments was selected in comparison with no-claims shipments. There were a total of 641 shipments used in the discriminant analysis, 170 of which were shipments on which claims had been filed. A random sample from this group would provide a C_{max} of .7348 shipments classified as no-claims. The pure chance proportion correctly classified if 26.52 percent of the shipments were classified as claims would be

$$P\ (\text{correct}) = (.2652)^2 + (.7348)^2 = .5602$$

Discriminant analysis prediction accuracy was 71.29 percent of grouped cases correctly classified. Therefore the discriminant function is not as good a prediction device as classifying all shipments as no-claims using the C_{max} criterion. The function did, however, do a somewhat better job than the chance proportion of correctly classified shipments when it is assumed that 26.52 percent of shipments would be classified as claims. Due to the high ratio of no-claims to claims shipments, discriminant analysis may not be a good prediction device.

Discriminant analysis may have value, however, in isolating those variables that are the best discriminators between the two groups—not for the purpose of predicting a claim but for the purpose of focusing management's attention toward those variables in an effort to control claims cost. Another purpose, of course, is to identify a group of discriminating variables for use in a multiple regression model for estimating cargo loss and damage expense.

MULTIPLE REGRESSION ANALYSIS

During the discriminant analysis phase of this study, 22 of 49 variables were selected as discriminators between a group of 471 no-claims shipments and 170 claims shipments. The purpose of performing the discriminant analysis was to identify discriminating variables between the two groups for management attention as well as to provide input variables for multiple regression analysis with the objective of predicting the amount of cargo loss and damage expense. The 22 variables were expanded to 25 when it was decided to create 0 or 1 dummy variable for the four types of traffic: shipper direct, shipper beyond, interline direct, and interline beyond. The dependent variable claims amount was regressed with the 25 resulting independent variables as follows: average weight per piece in shipment, date of shipment, carrier revenue, total pieces in shipment, rate, class, carton or box, crate, skid, pallet, can, originating area 4, total weight, number of rates, times handled, traffic type 1, traffic type 2, traffic type 3, traffic type 4, originating area 8, originating area 10, destination area 7, destination area 9, destination area 10, and fiber box.

For the regression, the single shipment cases were aggregated into monthly groups so that monthly totals could be obtained for the dependent and independent variables. A single case, then, for the regression analysis consisted of a month's total for each variable. The same 12 calendar months of 1975 that were included in the discriminant analysis were also used in the multiple regression analysis. Because there were only 12 cases and 25 variables, it was first necessary to regress claims amount with three groups of variables. For each of the three regressions, the independent variables explaining the greatest amount of variance were then run in two regression steps. Through this procedure all but 10 of the independent variables were eliminated from the analysis.

For the regression subprogram run on the computer, all the independent variables were entered in total for one regression analysis and also entered in forward stepwise inclusion procedures. This method is used when it is desired to "isolate a set of predictor variables that will yield an optimal prediction equation with as few terms as possible."[16] Using this approach three criteria are established: the number of variables to be entered into the equation, the minimum F ratio value the researcher is willing to accept for variables to be included in the equation, and tolerance.

The researcher may limit the equation to no more variables than the number desired. During the stepwise procedure, an F ratio is computed at each step as a test of statistical significance of a regression coefficient for the variables not in the equation. This ratio for any variable is the F value to be obtained if that variable were entered into the formula on the next step. In this study the default value in the program of .01 was used. This value places little restriction on the stepwise regression selection of variables.

Tolerance is defined as the proportion of the variance of an independent variable being considered for inclusion in the regression equation that is not explained by the variables already in the equation. This value will range from 0 to 1. "A tolerance of 0 implies that the variable is a perfect linear combination of the independent variables already in the equation." A tolerance of .70 would indicate that 70 percent of the variance of a new variable for entry would be unexplained by the variables already in the equation.[17] This criterion was also set at the default value, which is .001. This, of course, is not a strong barrier to entry.

The claim amount was regressed in a stepwise procedure on the ten independent variables. The resulting equation contained seven independent variables with unstandardized and standardized regression coefficients as follows:

X_i	Variable	Unstandardized Regression Coefficient	Standardized Regression Coefficient
X_1	Skid	477.7658	0.57491
X_2	Total weight	0.08151	1.44187
X_3	Number rates on bill	-30.11019	-0.23872
X_4	Carrier revenue	-0.73663	-1.10684
X_5	Class	1.03156	0.60488
X_6	Destination area 7	-151.09817	-0.26927
X_7	Average weight	-0.02235	-0.29436
	Constant	693.24031	

An examination of the above list and the absolute values of the standardized regression coefficients shows the contribution of the variables (X_i) in predicting the amount of claims expense. The major contributors are X_2, total weight; X_4, carrier revenue; and X_5, class followed by, in order of importance, X_1, skid; X_7, average weight; X_6, destination area 7; and X_3, number of rates on bill.

"The coefficient of multiple correlation, R^2 measures the proportion of the independent variable variance that is associated with or explained by the independent variables."[18] R^2 is calculated here by

$$R^2 = \frac{(Y^1 - \overline{Y})^2}{(Y - \overline{Y})^2}$$

where Y^1 is the predicted value of Y, Y is the observed value of Y, and $\overline{Y}$ is the mean of the observed values of Y. The regression program computes and prints the R^2 statistics. For the resulting regression equation in this study, the R^2 statistic was $R^2 = .94464$.

Test of the Equation

As a test of the overall goodness of fit of the regression equation, the null hypothesis that the multiple correlation is zero in the population from which the sample was drawn was tested. "This is equivalent to the null hypothesis that all K regression coefficients are equal to zero in the population."[19] Thus the null hypothesis tested and the alternative hypothesis were:

$$H_0 : B_1 = B_2 = B_k = 0$$

$$H_1 : B_k \neq 0$$

The F test statistic used to test this null hypothesis was computed as follows:

$$F = \frac{R^2/k}{(1 - R^2)(N - k - 1)} = \frac{.94464/7}{.05536/4} = 9.75$$

where R^2 = coefficient of determination, k = numbers of independent variables in the equation, and N = sample size. Reference to an F table shows the value of F with degrees of freedom of 7 and 4 at the .05 significance level to be 6.09. Therefore, the null hypothesis is rejected, and one may conclude that one or more of the regressive coefficients has an absolute value greater than zero.[20]

The hierarchical method of decomposition to test the coefficients B of the X_i independent variables was used.[21] Table 15 provides the hierarchical order and the associated statistics necessary for computing the F ratios for each coefficient. The null hypothesis tested is $H_0 : B_i = 0$; the alternate hypothesis is $H_1 = B_i \neq 0$. If the null hypothesis can be rejected at the .05 significance level, it is concluded that the B_i regression coefficient has a value greater than zero.

Computation of the F statistic for testing the null hypothesis that each independent variable's coefficient is equal to zero is as follows:

$$F = \frac{\text{Incremental sum of squares due to } X_i/1}{\text{Sum of squared residuals } / (N - k - 1)}$$

$$\text{Skid } F = \frac{.36922/1}{(1 - .94464)/4} = 26.67$$

Similar calculations were made for the other independent variables in the equation, and the results are depicted in Table 15.

The null hypothesis that the coefficient of a variable is equal to zero may be rejected only for the variable skid. The null hypothesis cannot be rejected for six of the independent variables included in the equation. This may or may not prove that the model may be

TABLE 15

Summary Table: Regression to Predict Claims Amount

Variable	Multiple R	R Square	R Square Change	Hand-Computed F	F at .05 Level of Significance
Skid	0.60764	0.36922	0.36922	26.67	21.20
Total weight	0.78269	0.61260	0.24337	17.58	21.20
Number rates	0.92231	0.85066	0.23806	17.20	21.20
Carrier revenue	0.94283	0.88790	0.03694	2.66	21.20
Class	0.95053	0.90352	0.01591	1.15	21.20
Destination area 7	0.95840	0.91853	0.01501	1.08	21.20
Average weight	0.97192	0.94464	0.02611	1.87	21.20

Source: Class I General Commodity Motor Carrier Sample.

biased and not a reliable predictor. However, the results indicate that further testing is necessary to preclude the possibility of bias in the model.

Direct Examination of Residuals

The regression equation was tested against the 12 calendar months of 1975. Comparison of predicted values with actual values and a plot of the standardized residuals are shown in Table 16.

An examination of the residuals is hampered somewhat by the small number of cases involved. However, the R^2 statistic of approximately .94 would show that a large amount of the variance in claims amount is explained by the independent variables in the equation. The residuals appear to be relatively small, only one lying as much as .5 standard deviation away from the residual mean, indicating a close fit of the equation to the data.

Further testing of the regression equation is necessary before it may be accepted as a predictor of cargo loss and damage expense. With the data available for testing goods, results appear. However,

TABLE 16

Residuals: Regression Equation to Predict Cargo Loss and Damage Expense, 12 Calendar Months, 1975

Month	Observed Claim/Amount	Predicted Claim/Amount	Residual	Plot of Standardized Residual -2.0 -1.0 0.0 1.0 2.0
1	1939.609	1979.973	-40.36469	*
2	423.5098	579.9944	-156.4838	*I
3	400.8896	615.0574	-214.1679	* I
4	635.7996	1011.343	-375.5432	* I
5	4304.574	4096.215	208.3583	I *
6	2212.908	2379.969	-167.0611	*I
7	1644.348	1076.114	568.2336	I *
8	2068.299	1767.210	301.0884	I *
9	2408.448	2648.636	-240.1883	* I
10	1089.289	830.6304	258.6582	I *
11	1960.009	1966.075	-6.065829	*
12	3410.219	3546.682	-136.4640	*I

Source: Class I General Commodity Motor Carrier Sample.

the number of cases on which all the necessary data are available is small. Perhaps a sample consisting of data gathered over a 60-month period of time would provide more insight into the long-term prediction capabilities of the model. Factors such as the influence of inflation and the effects of rate increases have not been taken into account, and in the long term such factors could affect the model's predictive ability. The model does show, however, that the use of discriminating variables selected through the use of discriminant analysis techniques may have merit when combined with multiple regression analysis. Such a technique should aid the researcher in efficiently and effectively reducing a large number of variables to a small, usable number for use in the regression equation.

During the analysis of the data collected in this sample study, a measure of the percent of shipments falling within a range of dollar value increments was established for shipments under 1,000 pounds. Expansion of the data into value per pound within selected weight brackets was accomplished. Claims ratios using weighted sample data were calculated for seven weight categories providing a means of analysis of cost within weight brackets. The importance of several ICC commodity code groups to cargo loss and damage expense within the motor carrier industry was tabulated and discussed. The sample data were used in multiple discriminant analysis and the discriminating variables found through discriminant analysis were entered into multiple regression analysis for the attempted prediction of cargo loss and damage expense.

NOTES

1. Regarding cross-subsidization of commodities, see Grant M. Davis and Linda J. Combs, "Value of Service Pricing," Transportation Journal 15 (Winter 1975), pp. 43-65 where an in-depth analysis of cross-subsidization is presented.

2. As a general rule, in the motor carrier industry, small shipments are defined as those weighing less than 500 pounds. However, some definitions would include all shipments weighing less than 1,000 pounds. See Sam Herold, Speech before ICC Practitioner 6th Annual Transportation Law Seminar (Washington, D.C., October 25-28, 1976).

3. Interstate Commerce Commission, Released Rates Application, No. MC-1228, Classification Ratings on Clothing, NOI, 349 ICC 211 (1975).

4. Interstate Commerce Commission, New Procedures in Motor Carrier Restructuring Proceedings Notice of Proposed Rule Making, Ex Parte No. MC-98 (1975).

5. Norman H. Nie et al., eds., Statistical Package for the Social Sciences (New York: McGraw-Hill, 1975), p. 184.

6. Interstate Commerce Commission, Quarterly Freight Loss and Damage Report for Quarter Ended September 30, 1975 (1975).

7. Herold, op. cit.

8. Ibid.

9. Middlewest Motor Freight Bureau, Traffic Study for the Year 1975 (Kansas City, Mo., 1976).

10. Ibid., study carrier's revenue on this traffic for the year 1975.

11. Ibid.

12. William Klecka, in Statistical Package for the Social Sciences, ed. Norman H. Nie et al. (New York: McGraw-Hill, 1975), p. 448.

13. Ibid.

14. Bruce Whittaker, director of Customer Service, Arkansas Best Freight System, telephone conversation, January 19, 1977.

15. Donald G. Morrison, "Discriminant Analysis," in Handbook of Marketing Research, ed. Robert Ferber (New York: McGraw-Hill, 1974), p. 2-446.

16. J. M. Kim and B. Kohout, in Statistical Package for the Social Sciences, ed. Norman H. Nie (New York: McGraw-Hill, 1975), p. 320.

17. Ibid., p. 346.

18. Henry J. Clacamp, "Correlation and Regression Methods," Handbook of Marketing Research, ed. Robert Ferber (New York: McGraw-Hill, 1974), p. 2-399.

19. Kim and Kohout, op. cit., p. 335.

20. Ibid., p. 336.

21. Ibid., p. 320.

6

IMPLICATIONS OF THE STUDY

The primary purpose of this thesis was to evaluate common carrier liability as it applies to motor common carriers of general commodities; to provide insight into cargo loss and damage expense and the potential for cost savings to the economy through a reduction of this expense on small shipments; and to attempt the development of models for predicting cargo loss and damage expense.

A major premise included in this research is the implication that the motor common carrier of general commodities possesses a unique inherent transportation advantage that must be preserved to meet the changing needs of commerce and for national defense. The common motor carrier of general commodities is a versatile, mobile, efficient mode of transportation that acts as the fulcrum for maintaining balance in the U.S. transportation system. Present regulation for the public interest must be geared toward strengthening the motor carrier and toward precaution of encroachment into areas that might impair the motor carrier's inherent advantage.

The entire study, with the possible exception of the discriminant and regression modeling, revolves around the small shipment. In Figure 1 it is shown that, on the average, 75 percent of motor carrier traffic was handled at revenues insufficient to cover cost. The compensatory traffic of motor carriers is composed, for the most part, of large shipments, which in fact subsidize the losses on small shipments. To compound the problem, motor carriers are losing some of this profitable traffic to private carriage and others.

An historic evolvement of common carrier liability as it applies to the common motor carrier of general commodities demonstrates that the motor carrier today is responsible for goods in its care to about the same degree as a common carrier in England during the genesis of common carrier law. Expanding economic needs, technology, and inflation appear to indicate that commodities today differ markedly from those commodities for which the common law developed. Now a wider range of value in goods is necessary to meet the demands of a growing population. Space age materials like plastics have different shipping characteristics from those of goods in the past. The conclusion could be drawn that common law liability may be outdated. The advantages of limiting that responsibility and restructuring freight rates on the small shipment according to a simplified less costly plan could be a significant contribution to the industry and the economy. Cost savings derived from such a plan would be achieved through reduced billing and claims costs.

The small shipment is a unique commodity, per se. When viewed in this perspective it possesses the characteristics that are used by the Interstate Commerce Commission as criteria for the approval of released rate proposals, including: there must be a wide range of value within the product group; the commodity must be susceptible to loss and damage; there must be a high ratio of claims to freight charges; there must be a higher frequency of claims within the commodity group than in other commodity groups; any proposed limited liability provisions must be comparable to relief granted other modes of transportation; and the relief sought by those proposing rate restructuring is required by competition. If this study is representative of all carriers, the tables and discussion in the dissertation would show that the small shipment as a unique commodity does meet the criteria for released rates.

CONTRIBUTIONS OF THE RESEARCH

The contributions of this thesis center upon the development of insight into common carrier liability for small shipments, the analysis of sample data to provide commodity value per pound information and claims ratio information, as well as the use of discriminant analysis and regression analysis as predictors of cargo loss and damage experience. Perhaps the principal contribution of this research is that useful claims information can be isolated through the study of a carrier's claims files and freight bill files. Claims ratio by weight bracket, value per pound frequency distributions, and claims cost savings at various released value limitations can be extracted and should be quite useful to the carrier as well as to the ICC. The methodology of selecting a large sample of claims rather than a random sample of all shipments provides for an overall smaller sample size at reasonable cost and does appear to contribute most of the information needed for the study of value per pound and dollar cost saving information at various released valuation proposals. Weighting factors are needed to arrive at statistics based on revenue.

Carrier Liability

The review of common carrier liability suggests a contrast between the motor carrier of today and the historic carrier for which the common law developed. The principal distinguishing characteristics between these two historic polarities are the structured continuity and competitiveness that are characteristics of today's motor truck carrier. Common law liability developed for the protection of shippers from the transient hauler of goods and later from the vagaries of monopoly. Motor truck common carriers today operate as going concerns of mostly a permanent nature and do not monopolize the transportation of freight. Perhaps suggestions in this research will provide some new insight into common carrier liability as it applies to motor truck common carriers of general commodities. A realignment of liability concepts may serve to decrease the cost of transportation in the nation as a whole.

Claims Cost Saving

A major implication of the study is the finding that on an aggregate basis the total cost saving as a percent of total revenue because of a limitation of liability in certain value per pound categories would not be large. The claims cost saving, however, when viewed as a percentage of that segment of revenue associated with small shipments was almost eight times greater than claims cost as a percentage of total revenue. So the cost savings, when viewed as a percentage of revenue from small shipments, is considerably more significant than when viewed as a percentage of revenue from all shipments. The principal thrust of a cost saving due to the limitation of liability would be toward the reduction of cost where it is most needed, in the area of the small shipment.

Value per Pound

The compilation of value per pound data into frequency distributions in increments of $1 per pound is not new. Such information, however, should be updated periodically due to inflation and technology. Any released rate proposal should include value per pound information for consideration by the ICC. An important finding in this research is that, for the study carrier, most shipments would continue to be fully covered by carrier liability at three different released valuation limits without the need for additional shipper insurance. For example, over 88 percent of shipments handled by the study carrier would have a value per pound measure of less than a $4 value per pound limit. This finding suggests that no inordinate hardship would be levied on shippers because of a released valuation ruling applicable to small shipments.

Claims Cost by Commodity

Study of claims cost by commodity suggests that most commodities would be fully covered by carrier liability even at released valuations of $3, $4, or $5 per pound. According to the sample data for the study carrier, about one-fourth of the ICC commodity groups accounted for 72 percent of the total dollar value of claims. Another interesting result of the study is that under a $4 per pound released rate valuation limit, two commodities accounted for 78.43 percent of total claims cost savings: commodity 2300, clothing except fur and fur trimmed, and commodity 3600, electrical machinery equipment and supplies, NOI. The results of the value per pound and claims by commodity analysis show that most shipments and most commodities would continue to be fully covered by carrier liability under a small shipment blanket-released rate plan.

Billing Cost Savings

An assumption was made arbitrarily that one-half the billing cost could be saved if a simplified rating plan not requiring extensive classification of shipments were approved. Applying this information to traffic study carrier information for 1975, it was determined that such a plan could save the economy for the study carriers alone $8,062,500. As a percent of total revenue, the savings would be 0.14 percent. Combining this savings with an estimated claims cost saving of .05 percent derived from the study carrier's sample data, a total savings of 0.19 percent of revenue could be achieved through a simplified billing plan accompanied by reduced liability. In this calculation, percentages from the sample study are used in conjunction with percentages from the traffic bureau study. However, the implication of an economic cost saving is embodied in the example.

Discriminant Analysis

The use of discriminant analysis as a classification technique for predicting claims shipments was found to be little better than chance when used with the sample data. Applying chance criteria to the total expected claims to total shipment ratio of the carrier indicated that discriminant analysis is not a good device for predicting claims occurrence. The use of the method, however, for selecting claims variables for study does appear to have merit. Using discriminant analysis, a carrier might, for example, gain insight into which terminals appear to differentiate more between claims shipments or no-claims shipments and whether or not the differentiation is due to that terminal's influence as a destination or originating terminal.

Multiple Regression Analysis

Multiple regression analysis was used in an attempt to predict the amount of cargo loss and damage expense. The data used in the model were monthly aggregated totals of the variables selected through discriminant analysis. Variables determined by the stepwise regression procedure to be the best predictors of cargo loss and damage expense amount were skid, total weight, number of rates on bill, carrier revenue, class, destination area 7, and average weight.

If the model is valid, the variables selected appear to be those that might have been selected on the basis of judgment with the possible exception of the packing variable skid. Skids are believed to contribute toward handling cost savings. The fact that this form of packing may contribute heavily toward cargo loss and damage expense may suggest a reassessment of the associated trade-off between claims cost and handling cost. In this study, skids contributed heavily to the regression equation. Further research is suggested in this area.

RECOMMENDATIONS FOR FURTHER RESEARCH

Sample Size and Value per Pound Studies

The sample size in this study was relatively small and applied to only one motor carrier. Even though the carrier's operation envelops a large geographical area, a large cross-sectional study of many carriers similar to the continuing traffic study should provide fairly conclusive results concerning the value per pound of shipments under 1,000 pounds, claims ratio by weight brackets, and possible billing savings through a released rating plan. Much of the information pertinent to such a study is already being collected from continuing traffic study carriers, with the possible exception of the value of shipments. The quarterly loss and damage claim report filed with the ICC could be expanded to include weight and value information as another base for accumulating data.

Such a study would require the gathering of value, commodity code, and revenue information at the time a claim is investigated and paid. The ICC report form could be expanded to include value. Concrete figures for evaluating proposed limits to carrier liability need to be established and the study need not be continuous in nature. After initiation of a restructuring plan, the study could be operated periodically to determine that limits of liability were still in reasonable limits for the maintenance of the system. Tables similar to those in this thesis would be prepared to substantiate any needed changes.

Studies of value and number of claims by commodity code should be included to isolate certain commodities for possible exclusion from the rating plan. The economic needs of the United States must be considered, and the commission must stress the common carrier concept for the benefit of the economy as a whole. Such exceptions to a simplified rating plan would certainly be few and most commodities needing additional liability coverage could probably be covered by the declaration of value in excess of the limit by the shipper and the payment of an additional rate for additional coverage.

Discriminant Analysis

Discriminant analysis as a predictor of cargo loss and damage on individual shipments was found to be no better than a classification of all shipments into the no-claims group. While this finding may be fairly conclusive, further research in this area is needed to provide knowledge of those variables related to cargo loss and damage. The data of such a study should include type of customer information, class, and cube, in addition to the variables used in this work. These variables should be collected as a matter of course during the everyday operation of the carrier if possible and be available from the freight bill file. Variables aimed at defining the age and condition of trailers used in linehaul and pickup and delivery operations should be included for the discriminant analysis and their effect on cargo loss and damage studied. Future research should include dummy variables for terminals for isolation to provide a more intense study of locational effects on cargo loss and damage.

Multiple Regression Analysis

Further research is needed in the development of a multiple regression model for predicting cargo loss and damage expense. The model in this study had an R^2 statistic of over .94 but the model conceivably could be biased. Additional research should be based on a sample consisting of possibly 60 cases or a five-year period in months. One or two years' test data should also be selected for testing the model. An inflationary weight should be provided through the use of the consumer's price index or the gross national product implicit price deflator to prevent long-range bias in the model. The regression analysis need not be limited to just the best predicting variables. It would appear that other variables may be used separately in multiple regression to ascertain relationships that could be meaningful to management. Additional variables that could be studied using regression procedures would include dummy variables for individual terminal locations and type of customer. Such a study could have significant impact on carrier claims prevention programs.

Finally, the ICC, based on this research, should consider released rates to maintain the common carrier system.

BIBLIOGRAPHY

Altman, Edward I. "Financial Ratios, Discriminant Analysis and the Reduction of Corporate Bankruptcy." Journal of Finance 23 (September 1968).

Armstrong, David H. "Focusing on Regulatory Issues." Public Utilities Fortnightly, August 27, 1970.

Bowersox, Donald J. Logistical Management. New York: Macmillan, 1974.

____, Edward W. Smykay, and Bernard J. LaLonde. Physical Distribution Management. 6th printing. New York: Macmillan, 1972.

Clacamp, Henry J. "Correlation and Regression Methods. In Handbook of Marketing Research. Edited by Robert Ferber. New York: McGraw-Hill, 1974.

Colquitt, Joseph C. The Art and Development of Freight Classification. Washington, D.C.: National Motor Freight Traffic Association, 1956.

Creedy, John A. "The Built-in Bias Against Efficiency Improvement in Transportation: What to Do About It." ICC Practitioners Journal 42, January-February 1975.

Davis, Grant M., Martin T. Farris, and Jack Holder, Jr. Management of Transportation Carriers. New York: Praeger, 1975.

Economic Research Committee of the Regular Common Carrier Conference. 1971 Cost/Revenue Analysis. Washington, D.C.: American Trucking Association, 1971.

Flood, Kenneth W. Traffic Management. Dubuque, Iowa: Brown, 1975.

Frear, Howard. "Rate Regulation Today." ICC Practitioners Journal, June 1966.

Herold, Samuel G. Speech before ICC Practitioners 6th Annual Transportation Law Seminar, October 25-28, 1976, Washington, D.C.

Interstate Commerce Commission. Investigation and Suspension Docket No. M22991, Classification Ratings Based on Density, 337 ICC 786.

____. Classification Ratings on Furniture, 177 ICC 5.

____. Dow Chemical Company v. Chesapeake and Ohio Railway Company et al., 306 ICC 404.

____. Investigation and Suspension Docket No. 7565, Iron and Steel Rings from Pittsburgh, Pa., to Cincinnati, Ohio. 1962.

____. Montgomery Ward & Co. v. Abilene & S. Ry. Co., 147 ICC 415.

____. New Procedures in Motor Carrier Revenue Proceedings, Ex Parte No. MC-82, 339 ICC 324.

____. Ex Parte No. MC-98, New Procedures in Motor Carrier Restructuring Proceedings, Notice of Proposed Rule Making. 1975.

____. Ex Parte MC-49, Released Rate Rules, National Motor Freight Classification, 316 ICC 499. 1962.

____. Released Rates Application No. MC-1228, Classification Ratings on Clothing, NOI, 349 ICC 211. 1975.

____. Released Ratings and Rates on Engines, 47 ICC 767. 1948.

____. Released Rates Order No. MC-920, Denying Released Rates Application No. MC-1408, All Shipments Weighing Less Than 300 Pounds. May 1976.

____. Released Rates Application No. MC-1282, Rocky Mountain Motor Traffic Bureau, Inc., Released Value Minimum Charges, 351 ICC 505. 1972.

____. Released Rates Order No. MC-917, Denying Released Rates Application No. MC-1399, Intermountain Tariff Bureau, Inc. May 1976.

____. Rock Island Chamber of Commerce v. Boston & A.R., 148 ICC 63.

____. Southern Class Rate Investigation, 100 ICC 602.

____. Wearing Apparel, Accessories, Piece Goods—Shulman, Inc., 321 ICC 1.

____. Quarterly Report of Freight Loss and Damage Claims Motor Schedules A, B and C. 1973.

____. Quarterly Freight Loss and Damage Claims for Quarter Ended September 30, 1975. 1975.

____. Terminal Property and Cargo Loss and Damage Expense Allocation, Supplement to Classes I and II Motor Carrier Annual Report Forms for the Cost Study Year 1974, ACC-43 (7/75). 1975.

____. 49 C.F.R. 1207 Uniform System of Accounts, Class I and Class II Common Carriers of Property. 1976.

Korodi, Miklos B. "Terminal Security—It's a Systems Job." Traffic World, April 7, 1975.

McKinley, A. H. "Pinpointing Loss and Damage." Distribution Worldwide, March 1972.

Mark, William, and Donald T. Kiser, eds. Corpus Juris Secundum. St. Paul: West, 1970.

Meyers, John R., Merton J. Peck, John Stenason, and Charles Zurick. The Economics of Competition in the Transportation Industries. Cambridge, Mass.: Harvard University Press, 1969.

Middle Atlantic Conference. Released Rates Application Seeking Released Valuation Rule for Application on All Commodity Rates and Charges on Shipments Weighing Less Than 1,000 Pounds. Middle Atlantic and New England Territories. 1975.

Middlewest Motor Freight Bureau. Traffic Study for Year 1975. Kansas City, Mo., 1976.

Morrison, Donald G. "Discriminant Analysis." In Handbook of Marketing Research. Edited by Robert Ferber. New York: McGraw-Hill, 1974.

Morton, Newton. "Common Law, Common Carriers and Their Transportation of Goods of Extraordinary Value." Paper. Kent State University, 1967.

National Motor Freight Claim Council. The Claims Councillor, December 1975.

Nie, Norman H., C. Hadlai Hull, Jean G. Jenkins, Karen Steinbrenner, and Dale H. Bent, eds. Statistical Package for the Social Sciences. New York: McGraw-Hill, 1975.

Noble, Jim. "In Motion Damage Costs Carriers Dearly, Claim Council Is Told." Transport Topics, July 5, 1976.

Parr, Gilbert J. "The Import of the Interstate Commerce Commission Studies on Railroad Freight Rates in the United States." ICC Practitioners Journal 42 (September-October 1975).

Salzano, Carlo J. "Why Not a Pocketbook Approach to Cargo Loss and Damage." Traffic World, April 7, 1975.

Sampson, Roy, and Martin T. Farris. Domestic Transportation: Practice, Theory, and Policy, 2nd ed. Boston: Houghton Mifflin, 1971.

Sigmon, Richard R. Miller's Law of Freight Loss and Damage Claims, 4th ed. Dubuque, Iowa: Brown, 1974.

Skulina, Thomas R. "Liability of a Carrier for Loss and Damage to Interstate Shipments." Cleveland Marquette Law Review, May 1968.

Taff, Charles A. Management of Physical Distribution and Transportation. Homewood, Ill.: Richard D. Irwin, 1972.

____. "Trends in Claims Against Truckers." Distribution World Wide. September 1971.

____. "UPS Asks ICC for Relief from Certain Weight Restrictions." Traffic World, November 29, 1976.

Whittaker, Bruce. Director of Customer Service, Arkansas Best Freight System, Fort Smith, Ark. 1976. Personal Interview.

ABOUT THE AUTHORS

GRANT M. DAVIS is currently the Oren Harris Professor of Transportation and a member of the Graduate Faculty in the University of Arkansas' College of Business Administration. He has considerable industrial experience with Ford Motor Company and the Mason and Dixon Lines in the fields of traffic, transportation, and distribution. He has published more than 90 major journal and technical articles in such journals as I.C.C. Practitioners' Journal, Transportation Journal, Traffic Quarterly, Quarterly Review of Economics and Business, and The Logistics Review. He is the author of The Department of Transportation (Lexington, Massachusetts: D. C. Heath, Series, 1970), Logistics Management (Lexington, Massachusetts: D. C. Heath, 1974), Rate Bureau and Antitrust Conflicts (New York: Praeger, 1975), Management of Transportation Carrier (New York: Praeger, 1975), and Transportation Regulation: A Pragmatic Assessment (Danville, Illinois: Interstate Press, 1976).

Dr. Davis has extensive consulting experience in the areas of business and government. He is an Interstate Commerce Commission Practitioner and a member of the Association of Interstate Commerce Commission's Bar, American Society of Traffic and Transportation, Delta Nu Alpha, Society of Logistics Engineers, American Economics Association, Southern Marketing Association, Beta Gamma Sigma, the Alabama Academy of Science, and many other groups.

Dr. Davis was named National Transportation Man-of-the-Year in 1971 by Delta Nu Alpha. He is listed in Outstanding Educators in America, Who's Who in the West, Personalities of the South, International Biography, Who's Who in the Southwest, and Contemporary Authors of America.

EUGENE H. SHEPARD is an assistant professor of accountancy at Florida Technological University, Orlando, Florida. He is a certified public accountant. Dr. Shepard spent over 20 years in wholesale distribution in the wholesale drug industry. He is a member of the American Society of Traffic and Transportation, The American Accountancy Association, and The American Institute of Certified Public Accountants.

Dr. Shepard received his BSBA in accounting from the University of Southern Mississippi, MS in accounting from Colorado State University, and Ph.D. in accounting from the University of Arkansas.

RELATED TITLES
Published by
Praeger Special Studies

INCREASING MOTOR CARRIER PRODUCTIVITY
Grant M. Davis
John E. Dillard, Jr.

LABOR RELATIONS IN A PUBLIC SERVICE INDUSTRY: Unions, Management, and the Public Interest in Mass Transit
Kenneth M. Jennings, Jr.
Jay A. Smith, Jr.
Earle C. Traynham, Jr.

PROBLEMS OF THE CARLESS
Robert E. Paaswell
Wilfred W. Recker